the Ultimate Little SHOOTER BOOK

Ray Foley

SOURCEBOOKS, INC.®
NAPERVILLE, ILLINOIS

D0288597

Copyright © 2001, 2005 by Ray Foley
Cover and internal design © 2005 by Sourcebooks, Inc.
Sourcebooks and the colophon are registered trademarks of Sourcebooks, Inc.

All rights reserved. No part of this book may be reproduced in any form or by any electronic or mechanical means including information storage and retrieval systems—except in the case of brief quotations embodied in critical articles or reviews—without permission in writing from its publisher, Sourcebooks, Inc.

This publication is designed to provide accurate and authoritative information in regard to the subject matter covered. It is sold with the understanding that the publisher is not engaged in rendering legal, accounting, or other professional service. If legal advice or other expert assistance is required, the services of a competent professional person should be sought.—*From a Declaration of Principles Jointly Adopted by a Committee of the American Bar Association and a Committee of Publishers and Associations*

All brand names and product names used in this book are trademarks, registered trademarks, or trade names of their respective holders. Sourcebooks, Inc., is not associated with any product or vendor in this book.

Some recipes contained herein may call for raw or undercooked eggs. Please consult with your physician prior to consumption.

The Author and Sourcebooks, Inc. shall have neither liability nor responsibility to any person or entity with respect to any loss, damage, or injury caused or alleged to be caused directly or indirectly by the information in this book.

Published by Sourcebooks, Inc.
P.O. Box 4410, Naperville, Illinois   60567-4410
(630) 961-3900
FAX: (630) 961-2168
www.sourcebooks.com

Originally published in 2001

Library of Congress Cataloging-in-Publication Data

Foley, Ray.
   The ultimate little shooter book / Ray Foley.
      p. cm.
   Rev. ed. of: Ultimate little shooter book II, 2001.
   ISBN 1-4022-0633-X (alk. paper)
   1. Alcoholic beverages. 2. Cocktails.   I. Foley, Ray. Ultimate little shooter book II.
II. Title.

TX951.F595 2005
641.8'74—dc22
                                                   2005017685

Printed and bound in Canada.
WC   10 9 8 7 6 5 4 3 2

Dedication

This book is dedicated to our son, Ryan Peter, the best shot we ever took!

Acknowledgments

Allied Domecq Spirits USA
Angostura International Ltd.
Anheuser-Busch, Inc., Diane Burnell
Austin, Nichols & Co., Inc
Bacardi USA, Inc.
Banta Book Group, Bob Christopher
Barton Incorporated
Branca Products Corporation
Brown-Forman Beverages Worldwide
Cairns & Associates, Inc.
Charles Jacquin et Cie., Inc. Patricia Bormann,
    John Cooper, Kevin O'Brien
Coco Lopez, Inc. Jose Suarez, R. Jake Jacobsen
Crillon Importers
Dozortsev & Sons Enterprises, Ltd.
Dunwoodie Communications, Greg Cohen
Finlandia Vodka Americas, Inc.
Heaven Hill Distilleries, Inc.
Jim Bean Brands Worldwide, Inc.
Kobrand Dorp
Kratz & Jesen, Inc. Christine Deussen, Alicia
    DiFolco
Major Peters Bloody Mary Mix
Manitowoc Ice, Inc., Larry Hagman
Marie Brizard Wines and Spirits, USA
Miller Brewing Company, Joan Zitzke
Mott's USA, Jeff Polisoto
National Cherry Board, Cheryl Kroupa
Niche Marketing
Remy Amerique, Robert Rentsch
Schieffelin & Somerset, Jeff Pogash
Seagram North America, Robert Dubin, Arthur

Shapiro
Skyy Spirits LLC
Robert Suffredini
Steve Baron Communications
The Baddish Group, Laura Baddish
The Good Group, Mark Bloom
The Gang at Maker's Mark
Todhunter International, Inc.
Top Shelf Marketing, George and Kelly Borrello
UDV North America
Vita Mix
Waring Products, Joan Gioiella

Special thanks to Jimmy Zazzali, Matt Wojciak, John Cowan, Michael Cammarano, Charles Chop, Marvin Solomon, the Rinaldi's (Millie and Anthony), plus Loretta Natiello, Dawn Jenny, and Erica DeWitte for putting this to paper. Also, to all those who submitted recipes to www. bartender.com and the readers of Bartender magazine.

A Short History of Shot Glasses

by Mark Pickvet

Tiny glass vessels were once filled with lead shot and were then used to clean and support quill pens. This origin of the word "shot" had its begin- nings in Europe. The shot glass is also an American term for a tiny drinking vessel used for serving whiskey in single measures. Before the widespread use of the word "shot" in the later nineteenth century, there were a variety of other terms used to describe them.

Dram glasses and firing glasses were popular in England dating back to the early eighteenth century. Dram glasses were cheaply made of thin metals and broke easily but were used heavily in the practice of dramming. Dramming involved drinking several small toasts of rum, gin, brandy, or whiskey in succession ordinarily in lodges, taverns, and even specialty dram shops. Firing glasses were stronger articles of thick glass, particularly the bottoms. They could withstand considerable abuse and were typically slammed up on the table after each successive toast. The resulting noise was comparable to that of a musket firing, hence the name "firing glass." In America, the first generation of tiny whiskey tumblers were referred to as toy whiskey tasters because they were so small (most had capacity of barely an ounce). They date back to the 1830s and were used for sampling whiskey.

One of the most significant eras in shot glass history began in the 1880s and lasted up to

Prohibition in 1919. The pre-Prohibition whiskey sample glass era consisted of clear or crystal shot-sized glasses with some form of advertising. Naturally the advertising was alcohol-related for proprietors, distillers, store-owners selling whiskey, pharmacists and doctors dispensing liquor, saloons, clubs, and so on. The word "sample" originated from the gimmick of salesmen, peddlers, and agents who offered free samples of the product that they were promoting. Other shot glasses were produced in cut crystal, oily carnival colors, and especially the variety of colors during the Depression era. A new style of shot glass was made during the 1920s and the 1930s; it was 2 7/8 inches tall, narrower, held exactly one ounce, and had an incredibly thick bottom. Some were so thick that the capacity for liquid was less than an ounce and they were often referred to as "cheaters."

Numerous toasts were added to shot glasses such as "Here's Looking at You," "Bottoms Up," "Down the Hatch," "Just a Swallow," and many others. In the post-Depression era, the decorated tumbler soon became the most popular medium for shot glass production. Machine-applied enamels and heat-transfers were cheaply fused to shot glasses in huge numbers. Shot glasses decorated with advertising, sports teams, Christmas and other holidays, plain patterns, and the thousands of tourist glasses have assailed the post-Depression era. Production of thick durable shot glasses for bar use has never wavered since the time of the firing glass.

Introduction

All recipes have been alphabetized for your convenience.

Techniques for Mixing

1. *Build:* Pour one liquor on top of the other per recipe.
2. *Layer:* Pour one liquor on top of the other using the back of a bar spoon or teaspoon.
3. *Shake and Strain:* Shake with ice and strain.

*We do not recommend flaming any shooter.

Publisher's Note: This book and the recipes contained herein are intended for those of a legal drinking age. Please drink responsibly and ensure you and your guests have a designated driver when consuming alcoholic beverages.

Shooters from A to Z

Aardvark
1/3 oz. Parfait Amour
1/3 oz. Tia Maria
1/3 oz. cream

ABC
1/2 oz. amaretto
1/2 oz. Baileys Irish Cream
1/2 oz. Cointreau

Build.

A-Bomb
1/4 oz. Kahlúa
1/4 oz. Fris vodka
1/4 oz. Baileys Irish Cream
1/4 oz. Tia Maria liqueur

Shake with ice and strain.

Absolut Aphrodisiac
1 raw oyster
1 oz. Absolut Peppar

Place in a shot glass. Add a splash of Tabasco sauce.

Absolut Firecracker

1 part grenadine
1 part Absolut Peppar
1 part blue curacao

In a shot glass, layer equal parts in the above order and let the fireworks begin!

Absolut in the Ocean

1/2 oz. Absolut vodka
1/2 oz. Cointreau
splash blue curacao

Andreas Grouzis
Skala Kefalonia, Greece

Absolut Nut

3/4 oz. Absolut vodka
3/4 oz. Frangelico

Shake with ice and strain.

Absolut Pepparmint

1 1/4 oz. Absolut Peppar
1/4 oz. Rumple Minze peppermint schnapps

Mix.

Absolut Quaalude

1/3 part Frangelico
1/3 part Baileys Irish Cream
1/3 part Absolut vodka

Shake with ice and strain.

Absolut Sex

1 1/4 oz. Absolut Kurant
1/2 oz. Midori melon liqueur
cranberry juice
7-Up

Fill with equal parts of cranberry juice and
7-Up in shot glass.

Absolut Stress

1/2 oz. Absolut vodka
1/4 oz. peach schnapps
1/2 oz. Malibu
splash cranberry juice
splash pineapple juice

Shake with ice and strain.

Absolut Testa Rossa

1 oz. Absolut vodka
1/2 oz. Campari

Absolut White Death

1/2 oz. Absolut vodka
1/2 oz. white crème de cacao
1/2 oz. Chambord

Shake with ice and strain.

Agean Shooter

3/4 oz. Metaxa brandy
1/3 oz. ouzo
1/3 oz. grenadine

Shake with ice and strain.

Affair

1 oz. strawberry schnapps
3/4 oz. cranberry juice
3/4 oz. orange juice

Stir with ice and strain into cordial glass.

African Violet

3/4 oz. green crème de menthe
3/4 oz. Frangelico

Build.

After 69 Shooter

1 shot Soi Soi Sant Neuf
1 shot Kahlua

Pour into cordial glass. Top with cream liqueur. You may want to use it before.

After Burner

3/4 oz. Hiram Walker peppermint schnapps
3/4 oz. Kahlua

Shake with ice and strain.

After Burner #2

3/4 oz. Tia Maria
3/4 oz. Hiram Walker peppermint schnapps

Build.

After Dinner Mint

1 oz. dark crème de cacao
1 1/2 oz. Baileys Irish Cream
splash green crème de menthe

Build.

After Eight

1/2 oz. Hiram Walker green crème de menthe
1/2 oz. Kahlúa
1/2 oz. cream

Layer. Serve in a 2 oz. shooter glass.

After Eight #2

1/3 Kahlúa
1/3 Baileys Irish Cream
1/3 white crème de menthe

Build.

After Five

1/3 Kahlúa
1/3 Baileys Irish Cream
1/3 Rumple Minze peppermint schnapps

Build.

After Five #2

1 part Baileys Irish Cream
1 part Rumple Minze peppermint schnapps

Build.

After Six

3/4 oz. Hiram Walker peppermint schnapps
3/4 oz. Carolans Irish Cream
splash Kahlúa

Serve chilled in a shooter glass.

Agent Orange

1/2 oz. Grand Marnier
1/2 oz. Myers's Original dark rum
1/2 oz. Tropicana orange juice
1/2 oz. sour mix

Shake with ice and strain.

Aggravation

1/2 oz. Teacher's scotch
1/2 oz. Kahlúa
3/4 oz. cream

Shake with ice and strain.

Alabama Nut Slammer

1 oz. Frangelico
1/4 oz. Southern Comfort

Christopher Dabbs
Homewood, AL

Alabama Slammer

1/4 oz. Stolichnaya vodka
1/4 oz. Disaronno amaretto
1/4 oz. Southern Comfort
splash orange juice
dash grenadine

Shake with ice and strain.

Alabama Slammer #2

1/2 oz. Southern Comfort
1/2 oz. vodka
1/2 oz. sloe gin
1/2 oz. amaretto
3 parts orange juice

Shake with ice and strain.

Alabama Slammer #3

1/4 Southern Comfort
1/4 amaretto
1/4 sloe gin
1/4 orange juice

Shake with ice and strain.

Alamo

1 1/2 oz. Southern Comfort
1/2 oz. grapefruit juice

Shake with ice and strain.

Alaskan Oil Slick

1 oz. Rumple Minze peppermint schnapps
1/2 oz. blue curacao
float Jagermeister

Shake with ice and strain.

Alaskan Oil Spill

3/4 oz. Rumple Minze peppermint
schnapps
3/4 oz. Jagermeister

Build.

Alice in Wonderland

1 oz. Cuervo tequila
1/4 oz. Tia Maria
1/4 oz. Grand Marnier

Shake with ice and strain.

All Fall Down Shooter

1 shot Monte Alban tequila
1 shot Myers's Original dark rum
1 shot Tia Maria

Shake with ice and strain.

Almond Joy

1/2 oz. amaretto
1/2 oz. dark crème de cacao
1/2 oz. vodka
1/2 oz. cream

Shake with ice and strain.

Almond Joy #2

1/2 oz. amaretto
1/2 oz. dark crème de cacao
1/4 oz. CoCo Lopez cream of coconut
1/4 oz. cream

Shake with ice and strain.

Almond Smash

1/2 oz. amaretto
1 oz. crème de almond
1 1/2 oz. 7-Up

Build.

Aloha Shooter

1/4 oz. amaretto
1/4 oz. Southern Comfort
1/4 oz. grenadine
1/4 oz. orange juice
1/2 oz. pineapple juice

Shake with ice and strain.

Alpine Breeze

1/2 oz. Myers's Original dark rum
1/2 oz. peppermint schnapps
1-2 dashes grenadine
1 oz. pineapple juice

Shake with ice and strain.

Altered States

1/3 oz. Kahlúa
1/3 oz. Baileys Irish Cream
1/3 oz. brandy

Alyce from Dallas Shooter

1 part Kahlúa
1 part Grand Marnier
1 part Monte Alban tequila

Build.

Amaretto Chill

Equal parts:
vodka
amaretto
lemonade mix
pineapple juice

Amberjack

1 part amaretto
1 part Jack Daniel's

Build.

American Dream

1/2 oz. Kahlúa
1/2 oz. amaretto
1/2 oz. Frangelico

Shake with ice and strain.

American Flag

1/2 oz. blue curacao
1/2 oz. cream
1/2 oz. grenadine

Layer in order.

Amigo Shooter

2/3 shot Monte Alban tequila
2/3 shot Kahlua
1 splash half & half

Blend and strain. Nutmeg/allspice garnish.

Amor

1 oz. Sauza Commemorativo tequila
1/2 oz. Hiram Walker orange curacao

Build.

Angel Bliss

1/4 oz. Wild Turkey
1/4 oz. Bacardi 151 rum
1/2 oz. blue curacao

Build.

Angel Wing

1 oz. white crème de cacao
1 oz. Baileys Irish Cream

Build.

Angel's Delight

1 part grenadine
1 part triple sec
1 part sloe gin
1 part light cream

Layer in order in cordial glass.

Angel's Kiss

1 1/2 oz. dark crème de cacao
dash heavy cream

Build. Garnish with cherry on toothpick.

Angel's Tip

1 shot dark crème de cacao

Float half & half on top.

Anti-Freeze

1/2 Midori melon liqueur
1/2 Smirnoff vodka

Build.

Anti-Freeze #2

1/2 Galliano
1/2 vodka

Serve as a shooter with a couple drops of blue curacao.

Anti-Freeze #3

1 oz. blue curacao
1/2 oz. spearmint schnapps
dash 7-Up

Shake with ice and strain. Top with 7-Up.

Anti-Freeze #4

1/2 green crème de menthe
1/2 vodka

Shake with ice and strain.

Apocalypse Now

1/3 oz. Baileys Irish Cream
1/3 oz. dry vermouth
1/3 oz. tequila

Apple & Spice Shooter

2/3 shot Applejack brandy
2 splashes half & half

Shake with ice and strain. Garnish with cinnamon.

Apple Delight

1/4 oz. amaretto
1/2 oz. apple schnapps
1/4 oz. vodka
1/4 oz. cranberry juice

Shake with ice and strain.

Apple Pie

3/4 oz. apple schnapps
1/2 oz. cinnamon schnapps

Build.

Apple Pie #2

vodka
apple juice
dash cinnamon

Apple Pie #3

2/3 shot apple schnapps
1/3 shot Frangelico

Top with dot of whipped cream. Garnish with allspice.

Apple Sensation 2000

1/2 oz. apple pucker
1/4 oz. Midori
1 1/2 oz. Stolichnaya
splash sweet & sour
splash cranberry juice

Matt Kay
Los Angeles, CA

Arctic Front

1 oz. Yukon Jack
1 oz. vodka

Shake with ice and strain.

Armadillo

1/2 oz. Kahlúa
1/2 oz. Disaronno amaretto
1/4 oz. Grand Marnier
1/4 oz. Bacardi 151 rum

Build.

Armpit

1 1/2 oz. Rumple Minze peppermint
  schnapps
cranberry juice
splash 7-Up

Shake with ice and strain. Top with 7-Up.

Asian Persuasion

1/2 oz. Midori
1/4 oz. Malibu
1/2 oz. Bacardi 151
splash pineapple juice
splash 7-Up

Athanie Leeviraphan
Stillwater, OK

Assassin

3/4 oz. Hiram Walker crème de banana
1/4 oz. Hiram Walker blue curacao
3/4 oz. Hiram Walker triple sec

Build.

Atomic Bomb Shooter

1 oz. bourbon
1/2 oz. tequila

Atomic Green

1/2 oz. Hiram Walker banana liqueur
1/2 oz. Midori melon liqueur
1/2 oz. Hiram Walker peach schnapps
1/4 oz. Fris vodka
1/4 oz. cream

Shake with ice and strain.

Attitude Adjustment

1 part ouzo liqueur
1 part Rumple Minze peppermint schnapps

Build.

Attitude Adjustment #2

3/4 oz. Baileys Irish Cream
3/4 oz. root beer schnapps
3/4 oz. Southern Comfort

Shake with ice and strain.

August Moon

1/2 oz. triple sec
1/2 oz. amaretto
1/2 oz. orange juice

Shake with ice and strain. Top with whipped cream.

Australian Lemondrop

1 1/2 oz. Stubbs Australian rum
3 oz. lemon juice
1 oz. sweet & sour mix
splash 7-Up

Build.

Australian Shooter

1 shot Jack Daniel's
splash cola

Build.

Avalanche

1/2 oz. Kahlúa
1/2 oz. Hiram Walker white crème de cacao
1/4 oz. Southern Comfort

Build.

Avalanche #2

1/3 Baileys Irish Cream
1/3 Jagermeister
1/3 spearmint schnapps

Look over your shoulder once and down the slope!

Chris Lima
Portsmouth, RI

Aviator

3/4 oz. Harveys Bristol cream sherry
3/4 oz. Dubonnet Blanc

Shake with ice and strain.

B.C.

1 part Absolut Citron vodka
1 part Kahlúa

Build.

B.J. Shooter

1/3 shot Baileys Irish Cream
1/3 shot Grand Marnier

Build.

B.V.B.

1/2 oz. butterscotch schnapps
1/2 oz. Absolut vodka
1/2 oz. Baileys Irish Cream

Float Absolut and Baileys over butterscotch.

Jimmy Oppel
Bobby Valentine's Sports Gallery Café
Middletown, RI

B-12

2/3 oz. Baileys Irish Cream
1/3 oz. Grand Marnier

Build.

B-26

1 part Kahlúa
1 part Carolans Irish Cream
1 part Hiram Walker triple sec

Shake with ice and strain.

B-51 in Flight

Kahlúa
Baileys Irish Cream
Bacardi 151 rum

Equal parts. Build.

B-52

1/2 oz. Kahlúa
1/2 oz. Baileys Irish Cream
1/4 oz. Grand Marnier
1/4 oz. Absolut vodka

Build. Drink through soda straw from bottom up.

B-52 with Bombay Doors

1/2 oz. Kahlúa
1/2 oz. Baileys Irish Cream
1/2 oz. Grand Marnier
1/2 oz. Bombay gin

Build.

B-54

1/3 shot Kahlúa
1/3 shot Baileys Irish Cream
1/3 shot Disaronno amaretto

Build.

B-69

1/4 oz. Kahlúa
1/4 oz. Baileys Irish Cream
1/4 oz. Grand Marnier
1/4 oz. butterscotch schnapps

Robin Norwood
Daphne, AL

Baby Ruth

1/2 Frangelico
1/2 vodka
2-3 peanuts

Build. Add peanuts.

Bachelor's Surprise

1/3 oz. Kahlúa
1/3 oz. white crème de cacao
1/3 oz. Southern Comfort

Back Draft

1 oz. Jose Cuervo 1800 tequila
1/2 oz. Grand Marnier
4 dashes Cholula hot sauce, let settle to
  the bottom

Steve Meyers
Southampton, NY

Back in Black

1 part Tia Maria
1 part Chambord

Build.

Bad Attitude

1/4 oz. Southern Comfort
1/4 oz. Absolut Citron vodka
1/4 oz. sloe gin
1/4 oz. amaretto
splash sour mix
7-Up
cranberry juice

Shake all but 7-Up. Top with 7-Up.

Debbie Douglas
Ducky's Bar
Pontiac, MI

Bad Sting

1/2 oz. anisette
1/2 oz. Grand Marnier
1/2 oz. Cuervo tequila
splash grenadine

Build.

Bah Humbug

1/2 oz. Southern Comfort
1/2 oz. amaretto
1/2 oz. orange juice
1/2 oz. cranberry juice

Shake with ice and strain.

Bahama Nut

3/4 oz. Nassau Royale liqueur
3/4 oz. Frangelico

Build.

Baileys Bomber

3/4 oz. Baileys Irish Cream
1/2 oz. J&B scotch

Build.

Bald Eagle

1 3/4 oz. Monte Alban tequila

Float peppermint schnapps.

Baileys Comet

1/2 oz. Baileys Irish Cream
1/2 oz. Kahlúa
1/2 oz. vodka
dash half & half
splash soda

Shake with ice and strain. Top with splash of soda.

Ball Bearing

1 1/4 oz. champagne
1/4 oz. Cherry Marnier

Build.

Bambi

3/4 oz. Kahlúa
1 1/4 oz. Baileys Irish Cream
splash Courvoisier

Check your site and shoot! Delicious sipping on the rocks too.

Jan DeBenedictis
Millis, MA

Bambino

1/2 oz. Disaronno amaretto
1/2 oz. cream
1/2 oz. Stolichnaya vodka

Shake with ice and strain.

Banana Bliss

1 oz. crème de banana
1/2 oz. cognac

Banana Boat

1/2 oz. Tia Maria
1/4 oz. Kahlúa
1/4 oz. Hiram Walker peppermint schnapps
1/4 oz. Meyers's rum cream

Build.

Banana Boat #2

3/4 oz. Malibu
3/4 oz. banana liqueur
1/2 oz. pineapple juice

Shake with ice and strain.

Banana Boat #3

1/3 shot Kahlúa
1/3 shot Tia Maria
1/3 shot Hiram Walker peppermint
   schnapps
float Baileys Irish Cream

Build.

Banana Boomer

3/4 oz. Puerto Rican rum
1/2 oz. Hiram Walker banana liqueur
3/4 oz. half orange & pineapple juice

Shake with ice, mix, and strain.

Banana Buca

1/2 oz. Romana sambuca
1/2 oz. crème de banana
1/2 oz. orange juice

Shake with ice and strain.

Banana Popsicle

1/2 oz. Frïs vodka
1/2 oz. Hiram Walker crème de banana
1/2 oz. orange juice

Shake with ice and strain.

Banana Sandwich

1/2 oz. Kahlúa
1/4 oz. crème de banana
1/4 oz. Myers's rum cream
1/4 oz. cream

Shake with ice and strain.

Banana Slip

1 1/4 oz. crème de banana
1 1/4 oz. Baileys Irish Cream

Layer in order in cordial glass.

Banana Split

1/2 oz. Hiram Walker crème de banana
1/2 oz. Hiram Walker crème de almond
1/4 oz. Kahlúa
1/2 oz. cream

Shake with ice and strain.

Banana Split #2

1 part Kahlúa
1 part Malibu
2 parts crème de banana
splash pineapple juice

Shake with ice and strain.

The Riverhouse/Club Bimini
Brielle, NJ

Banana Surfer

1/2 oz. Malibu
1/2 oz. banana liqueur
1/2 oz. cream

Shake with ice and strain.

Bananarama

1 oz. banana liqueur
1/2 oz. Bacardi rum
1/4 oz. orange juice
1/4 oz. pineapple juice

Shake with ice and strain.

Bananarama #2

1/2 oz. Kahlúa
1/2 oz. Hiram Walker amaretto
1/2 oz. Hiram Walker crème de banana
1/4 oz. cream

Shake with ice and strain.

Banshee

1 oz. crème de banana
1/2 oz. white crème de cacao

Shake with ice and strain.

Barnumenthe & Baileys

1 oz. Baileys Irish Cream
1/4 oz. Hiram Walker white crème de
  menthe

Build.

Bart Simpson

1/2 oz. Malibu
1/2 oz. Midori melon liqueur
1/2 oz. Smirnoff vodka

Shake with ice and strain.

Bart Simpson #2

3/4 oz. Hiram Walker CocoRhum
3/4 oz. Hiram Walker amaretto
3/4 oz. Hiram Walker crème de banana
1/4 oz. cream

Layer in order given, float cream on top.

Bartender on the Beach at Sunset

1 1/4 oz. Finlandia cranberry vodka
1/4 oz. Chambord
1/4 oz. Midori melon liqueur
2 oz. pineapple juice

Shake with ice.

Bazooka Shooter

1 oz. Southern Comfort
1/2 oz. crème de banana
dash grenadine
splash half & half

Shake with ice and strain.

B-Day

1/2 oz. Hiram Walker amaretto
1/2 oz. Kahlúa
1/2 oz. Grand Marnier
1/2 oz. cream

Shake with ice and strain.

Beach Ball

1/2 oz. Malibu
1/2 oz. blueberry schnapps
1/2 oz. pineapple juice

Shake with ice and strain.

Beach Bum

3/4 oz. Midori melon liqueur
3/4 oz. Finlandia vodka
1/2 oz. cranberry juice

Shake with ice and strain.

Beached Whale

1/2 oz. white crème de cacao
1/2 oz. Cointreau
1 oz. advocaat

Beam Me Up Scotty

1/2 oz. Kahlúa
1/2 oz. crème de banana
1/2 oz. Baileys Irish Cream

Build.

Bear Hug

1/2 oz. Kahlúa
1/2 oz. Romana sambuca
1/2 oz. Grand Marnier

Build.

Beauty and the Beast

1 oz. Jagermeister, cold
1 oz. Tequila Rose, cold

Kevin Worth
Goshen, NY

Beef on the Beach

1 oz. Beefeater gin
1/2 oz. peach schnapps
1/2 oz. cranberry juice
1/2 oz. pineapple juice

Joe Garza, Jr.
Fresno, CA

Beef and Schoenauer

1 1/2 oz. Shoenauer Apfel schnapps, chilled

Serve in a shot glass with your favorite beer on the side.

Beetlejuice

1/2 oz. amaretto
1/2 oz. vodka
1/2 oz. Midori
1/2 oz. cranberry juice

Bend Me Over

1 oz. Hiram Walker amaretto
3/4 oz. pineapple juice
1/4 oz. sour mix

Shake with ice and strain.

38

Bengali Driving School

1 1/2 oz. Midori melon liqueur
1/8 oz. Stolichnaya Razberi vodka
splash Rose's lime juice

Mix in tumbler and strain into shot glass. Place a cherry without the stem in shot glass. Viewed from above, the shooter resembles the flag of Bangladesh.

Chris Wertz
New York, NY

Berry Berry

1/2 oz. cherry brandy
1/2 oz. Chambord
1/2 oz. orange juice

Shake with ice and strain.

Berry Goldwater

1 oz. Der Lachs Goldwasser
1 1/2 oz. Echte Kroatzbeere blackberry
   liqueur

Build.

Berry Nuts

1/2 oz. Frangelico
1/2 oz. Disaronno amaretto
1/2 oz. Chambord
1/2 oz. Baileys Irish Cream

Build.

Mary Bellmer
Fenders—Turf Inn
Albany, NY

Berry Patch

1/2 oz. blueberry schnapps
1/2 oz. raspberry schnapps
1/2 oz. strawberry schnapps
1 splash orange juice

Shake with ice and strain.

Between the Sheets

1 part Bacardi rum
1 part brandy
1 part triple sec
2 parts sour mix

Shake with ice and strain.

Big F Shooter

1/3 Sambuca Molinari anisette liqueur
1/3 peppermint schnapps
2/3 Bacardi 151 rum

Build.

Big Mo Shooter

1/6 Baileys Irish Cream
1/6 Kahlúa
1/6 Absolut vodka
1/6 dark crème de cacao
1/6 Disaronno amaretto
1/6 Frangelico

Shake with ice and strain.

Bikini

3/4 oz. strawberry schnapps
3/4 oz. Grand Marnier
3/4 oz. vodka

Build.

Bikini Line

1/2 oz. Chambord
1/2 oz. Tia Maria
1/2 oz. vodka
1 splash pineapple juice

Shake with ice and strain.

Bite the Bullet

3/4 oz. tequila
splash Tabasco
3/4 oz. Goldschlager cinnamon schnapps

Black and Blue

1 oz. Romana sambuca
3/4 oz. Kahlúa

George P. Gintoli
Bridgeport, CT

Black Banana

3/4 oz. Kahlúa
3/4 oz. Hiram Walker crème de banana
3/4 oz. Frïs vodka

Build.

Black Blitzer

1/2 Black Haus blackberry schnapps
1/2 lemon blitzer
splash cranberry juice

Marybeth & Becky Hill
West Chester, OH

Black Bull

3/4 oz. tequila
3/4 oz. Kahlúa

Shake with ice and strain.

Black Cat

1/2 oz. Kahlúa
1/2 oz. apricot brandy
1/2 oz. ouzo

Build.

Black Death

1/2 oz. Bacardi 151 rum
1/2 oz. Kahlúa
1/2 oz. Southern Comfort
1/2 oz. Romana sambuca

Build.

Kevin Church
Las Vegas Cue Club
Las Vegas, NV

Black Devil Shooter

1 oz. dark rum
1 1/2 oz. crème de menthe

Black Eye

1/3 oz. vodka
1/3 oz. blackberry schnapps
1/3 oz. Rose's lime juice

Shake with ice and strain.

Black Forest

1/2 oz. blackberry brandy
1 oz. Wild Turkey

Shake with ice and strain.

Black Gold

3/4 oz. Goldschlager cinnamon schnapps
1/2 oz. Romana black sambuca

Pour Romana into ice-cold Goldschlager.

Black Jack Schlack

1 oz. Myers's Original dark rum
1 oz. Midori melon liqueur
splash cola

Shake with ice and strain. Top with cola.

Black Jelly Bean

1 1/2 oz. Chambord

Float Romana sambuca on top.

Black Mass

1/2 oz. Kahlúa
1/2 oz. Romana sambuca
1/2 oz. Bacardi 151 rum

Build.

Black Pearl

1/2 oz. Hiram Walker blackberry flavored
  brandy
1 oz. Hiram Walker peach schnapps

Shake with ice and strain.

Black Peppar

1 1/4 oz. Absolut Peppar vodka
1/4 oz. Hiram Walker blackberry flavored
  brandy

Shake with ice and strain.

Black Tie

1 part Opal Nera
2 parts Kahlúa

Shake with ice and strain.

Black-Eyed Susan

1 oz. Absolut Citron vodka
1/4 oz. orange juice
1/4 oz. pineapple juice

Shake with ice and strain.

Blackout

1 part Romana sambuca
1 part Della Notte
1 part Kahlúa

Mix with ice, strain, and serve.

Black-Out Shooter

2/3 shot Tanqueray gin
2/3 shot blackberry brandy
splash Rose's lime juice

Shake with ice and strain.

Bleeding Heart

1 1/4 oz. Finlandia cranberry vodka
1/2 oz. Baileys Irish Cream

Shake with ice and strain.

Blitzkrieg Shooter

1 1/2 oz. Rumple Minze peppermint
   schnapps
splash Bacardi 151 rum

Serve chilled.

Blood Clot Shooter

1 1/2 oz. Bacardi 151 rum
dash grenadine
float half & half

Blood Rush

1 1/2 oz. cherry brandy
1 oz. vodka

Build.

Bloody Brain

1 1/2 oz. strawberry schnapps
1 1/2 oz. Baileys Irish Cream
dash grenadine

Shake with ice and strain.

Bloody Caesar

1 littleneck clam
1 oz. Frïs vodka
1/2 oz. tomato juice
2 drops Worcestershire sauce
2 drops Tabasco sauce
dash horseradish celery salt

Put clam in bottom of shot glass. Add Worcestershire sauce, Tabasco, and horseradish. Add vodka and tomato juice. Sprinkle celery salt and garnish with a small lime wedge.

Bloody Russian

Equal parts:
  Absolut Peppar
  cocktail sauce

Fill shooter half way with cocktail sauce. Fill rest of shooter with Absolut Peppar.

Greg May
Livermore, CA

Blow Job

1 part Kahlúa
1 part Disaronno amaretto or Frangelico
1 part Baileys Irish Cream

Shake with ice and strain. Top with whipped cream.

Blow Job #2

1/2 oz. Kahlúa
1/2 oz. Baileys Irish Cream
1/2 oz. Absolut vodka
whipped cream

Build. Top with whipped cream as needed. Shoot without using hands.

Blue Angel

1 oz. Hiram Walker blue curacao
1 oz. orange juice

Shake with ice and strain.

Blue Bayou

1/2 oz. blue curacao
1/2 oz. Licor 43
1/2 oz. pineapple juice

Shake with ice and strain.

Blue Blood

1 1/2 oz. Royalty vodka
1/2 oz. blue curacao

Mark Schwartz
Rockaway, NJ

Blue Bombay

1 oz. Bombay Sapphire gin
1/4 oz. blue curacao

Shake with ice and strain.

Blue Carnation

1/2 oz. white crème de menthe
1/2 oz. blue curacao
3/4 oz. cream

Shake with ice and strain.

Blue Flame

1 oz. Liquore Galliano
1/4 oz. Bacardi 151 rum

Build.

Blue Fox

1 oz. blue curacao
1 oz. Southern Comfort

Build.

Blue Hawaiian

3/4 oz. Malibu
1/4 oz. white crème de cacao
1/4 oz. blue curacao
1/4 oz. pineapple juice
1/4 oz. orange juice

Shake with ice and strain.

Blue Ice

1 oz. vodka
1/8 oz. blue curacao
3/4 oz. sour mix
splash Rose's lime juice

Shake with ice and strain.

Ali
Ski Bar
New York, NY

Blue Kamakazi

1 1/2 oz. Finlandia vodka
1/8 oz. blue curacao
splash Rose's lime juice

Shake with ice and strain.

Blue Lemonade

1 oz. Absolut Citron
1/4 oz. blue curacao
1/4 oz. sour mix

Shake with ice and strain.

Blue Marlin

1 oz. Bacardi light rum
1/2 oz. blue curacao
1 oz. lime juice

Stir with ice and strain.

Blue Monday

1 dash blue curacao
1/4 oz. Grand Marnier
1 oz. vodka

Shake with ice and strain.

Blue Moon

1 1/2 oz. blueberry schnapps
dash blue curacao

Shake with ice and strain. Top with dash of
sour mix.

Blue Moon #2

1/2 oz. champagne
1/2 oz. blue curacao
1/2 oz. orange juice

Build.

Blue Motorcycle

1/2 oz. Beefeater gin
1/2 oz. Bacardi rum
1/4 oz. Frïs vodka
1/4 oz. Hiram Walker blue curacao
dash sour mix

Shake with ice and strain. Top with dash of
ginger ale.

Blue Oil Slick

1 oz. Frïs vodka
1/2 oz. Hiram Walker blue curacao
1/2 oz. Tia Maria

Shake with ice and strain.

Blue Popper

3/4 oz. tequila
splash Tabasco
1 oz. Hiram Walker blue curacao

Shake with ice and strain.

Blue Whale

1/2 oz. blue curacao
3/4 oz. peach schnapps
dash sweet & sour mix
dash club soda

Shake with ice and strain. Top with club soda.

Blue Whale #2

3/4 oz. Myers's Original dark rum
3/4 oz. blue curacao
1/2 oz. pineapple juice

Build.

Bluebeard

1/2 oz. blueberry schnapps
1 1/2 oz. vodka

Build.

Blueberry Cheesecake

1/2 oz. blueberry schnapps
1/2 oz. Disaronno amaretto
1/2 oz. Baileys Irish Cream

Build.

Blueberry Lemonade

1/2 oz. blueberry schnapps
1/2 oz. vodka
1/4 oz. sour mix
1/4 oz. cranberry juice

Shake with ice and strain.

Bluesberry

3/4 oz. Chambord
3/4 oz. blue curacao
1 oz. cream

Shake with ice and strain.

Blushin' Russian Shooter

1 oz. Stolichnaya vodka
1 oz. Kahlúa
half & half
Disaronno amaretto

Shake with ice and strain. Float Disaronno amaretto.

Blushing Bride

peach schnapps
wildberry schnapps
cranberry juice
7-Up

Equal parts. Build.

Walker & Linda Calvert
Calvert's Inn
Livingston, WI

Bob Marley

1 part peppermint schnapps
1 part Myers's Original dark rum

Build.

Bocci Ball

3/4 oz. Disaronno amaretto
3/4 oz. Stolichnaya vodka
1/2 oz. orange juice

Shake with ice and strain.

Bollweevil

1/2 oz. Old Grand Dad
1/2 oz. Southern Comfort
1/2 oz. blackberry brandy

Shake with ice and strain.

Bomber Shooter

1/3 oz. Disaronno amaretto
1/3 oz. Absolut vodka
2 splashes pineapple juice

Shake with ice and strain.

Bong Water

Equal parts:
    Southern Comfort
    Chambord
    amaretto
    Midori
splash pineapple juice
splash Sprite
splash Coke

Al Jacobson
Taylors Island, MD

Bonzai Pipeline

1/2 oz. Absolut vodka
1 oz. tropical fruit schnapps

Stir with ice and strain.

Booger

1 oz. Frïs vodka
1/2 oz. Midori melon liqueur
1/2 oz. Malibu
pineapple juice

Shake with ice and strain.

Boomer Shooter

3/4 oz. apricot brandy
3/4 oz. Monte Alban tequila
1/2 splash orange juice
1/2 splash sour mix

Shake with ice and strain.

Border Conflict Shooter

3/4 oz. Stolichnaya vodka
3/4 oz. Rumple Minze peppermint
  schnapps
splash grenadine

Stir and strain.

Born Free

1/2 oz. Wild Spirit
1 oz. Malibu

Shake with ice and strain.

Bourbon Street

3/4 oz. bourbon
3/4 oz. Disaronno amaretto

Build.

Boxer Shorts

1 oz. Finlandia vodka
1 oz. Rumple Minze peppermint schnapps

Build.

Brain

3/4 oz. Carolans Irish Cream
1/2 oz. Hiram Walker peach schnapps
1/2 oz. Hiram Walker strawberry schnapps

Build.

Brain #2

1 oz. Southern Comfort
1/3 oz. triple sec
1/3 oz. Baileys Irish Cream

Shake with ice and strain.

Brain Fart

1/2 oz. peach schnapps
1/2 oz. Baileys Irish Cream (floated)
dash Kahlúa
dash Crown Royal
2 dashes grenadine

Josh Walter
Nampa, ID

Brain Hemorrhage

3/4 oz. peach schnapps
1/2 oz. Baileys Irish Cream
drop grenadine

Build. Add 1 drop grenadine in center.

Brain Teaser

1/3 oz. amaretto
1/3 oz. sloe gin
1/3 oz. Baileys Irish Cream

Brandy Brainfreeze

1 1/2 oz. E & J brandy
3/4 cup strawberry daiquiri mix
1/2 cup ice

Blend. Top with a splash of cherry brandy.
Serve in shot glasses.

Rory L. Chatman
Norfolk, VA

Brave Bull

1 part Jose Cuervo tequila
1 part Kahlúa

Build.

Brighton Beach Hot Dog

1 1/2 oz. Stolichnaya Pertsovka
8 oz. Red Dog beer

Drop shot glass full of Pertsovka into an 8 oz. glass of Red Dog.

Broken Leg

3/4 oz. Hiram Walker peppermint schnapps
3/4 oz. Canadian Club whiskey

Shake with ice and strain.

Brown Cow

1 oz. dark crème de cacao
3/4 oz. triple sec
1/4 oz. cream

Shake with ice and strain.

Brown Cow #2

3/4 oz. white crème de cacao
3/4 oz. dark crème de cacao
1/2 oz. cream

Shake with ice and strain.

Brown Squirrel

1/2 oz. Hiram Walker dark crème de cacao
1/2 oz. Hiram Walker amaretto
1/4 oz. cream

Shake with ice and strain.

Bubble Gum

1/2 oz. Midori melon liqueur
1/2 oz. Frïs vodka
1/2 oz. Hiram Walker crème de banana
1/2 oz. orange juice

Shake with ice and strain.

Bubble Gum #2

1 oz. Finlandia cranberry vodka
1/4 oz. peach schnapps
1/4 oz. crème de banana
1 oz. orange juice

Shake with ice and strain.

Bubble Gum #3

3/4 oz. vodka
1/4 oz. banana liqueur
1/4 oz. peach schnapps
1 oz. orange juice

Shake with ice and strain.

Bubble Gum #4

1/2 oz. crème de banana
1/2 oz. Midori melon liqueur
1/4 oz. vodka
1/4 oz. grenadine
1/4 oz. orange juice
1/4 oz. sour mix

Shake with ice and strain.

Bubble Gum #5

3/4 oz. Southern Comfort
3/4 oz. blackberry brandy
1/2 oz. grenadine
cream

Shake with ice and strain.

Bucking Bronco

1 oz. Southern Comfort
1/2 oz. tequila

Build.

Buffalo Sweat

1 1/2 oz. bourbon
dash Tabasco sauce

Pour bourbon into a shot glass. Add a dash
of Tabasco.

Bull's Breath

1 part tequila
splash Tabasco
1 part cranberry juice

Anne Wilson
Wall, NJ

Burning Bush Shooter

1 shot Monte Alban tequila
1 dash Tabasco sauce

Build.

Bushwacker

1 oz. Baileys Irish Cream
1 oz. Jameson Irish whiskey

Build.

Busted Cherry

1/2 oz. Kahlúa
1/2 oz. cherry brandy
1/2 oz. cream

Build.

Butter Barrel Shooters

1 oz. DeKuyper root beer schnapps
1 oz. DeKuyper Buttershots
1 oz. A&W root beer soda

Angie Stockton
Harford, MI

Butterball

3/4 oz. butterscotch schnapps
1/2 oz. Grand Marnier

Build.

Buttery Jager Ripple

1/3 Jagermeister
1/3 Baileys Irish Cream
1/3 butterscotch schnapps

Shake with ice and strain.

Buttery Nipple

3/4 oz. butterscotch schnapps
3/4 oz. Baileys Irish Cream

Build.

Butt-Kicker

1/2 oz. Smirnoff vodka
3/4 oz. Chambord
3/4 oz. Malibu rum
splash pineapple juice

Wayne Sparks & Jean Marie Pietro
Carney's Pt., NJ

Buzzard's Breath

1/2 oz. Disaronno amaretto
1/2 oz. Rumple Minze peppermint schnapps
1/2 oz. Kahlúa

Stir with ice and strain.

C.B.

1 1/4 oz. Finlandia cranberry vodka
1/4 oz. blueberry schnapps
1/8 oz. triple sec

Shake with ice and strain.

Ca-Ca

1/4 oz. café royale
1/4 oz. anisette
1/4 oz. cherry brandy
1/4 oz. amaretto

Cactus Blue

1/2 oz. DeKuyper cactus juice liqueur
1/2 oz. DeKuyper blue curacao

Build.

Cactus Fever

1 1/2 oz. DeKuyper cactus juice liqueur

Pour cactus juice into a shot glass. Add salt and lime to taste.

California Kazi

3/4 oz. vodka
1/4 oz. triple sec
1/4 oz. Grand Marnier
1/4 oz. Rose's lime juice

Shake with ice and strain.

California Root Beer Shooter

1 oz. Kahlúa
1/2 oz. Liquore Galliano
cola

Shake with ice and strain. Top with cola.

California Shot

3/4 oz. Baileys Irish Cream
3/4 oz. Cuervo Gold tequila
splash coffee

Build.

Sam the Surfer
Santa Monica, CA

California Sizzler

1 part brandy
2 parts Malibu
2 parts orange juice

Build.

Canadian Boot

1 1/2 oz. Yukon Jack
1/2 oz. Disaronno amaretto

Craig Angel
Upland, CA

Candy Apple

3/4 oz. Hiram Walker apple schnapps
3/4 oz. Hiram Walker cinnamon schnapps
1/2 oz. cranberry juice

Shake with ice and strain.

Candy Ass

3/4 oz. Chambord
3/4 oz. Mozart chocolate liqueur

Shake with ice and strain.

Candy Cane

1 oz. Hiram Walker peppermint schnapps
1 oz. Hiram Walker cherry flavored
  brandy

Shake with ice and strain.

Cantaloupe

1/2 oz. strawberry brandy
1/2 oz. Licor 43
1/2 oz. orange juice

Shake with ice and strain.

Cape Cod Shooter

1 oz. vodka
1/2 oz. cranberry juice

Shake with ice and strain.

Capri

3/4 oz. white crème de cacao
3/4 oz. crème de banana
3/4 oz. light cream

Shake with ice and strain into cordial glass.

Capt. Cotton Candy

1 oz. Captain Morgan Silver rum
1 oz. Collins mix
1/2 oz. cranberry juice

Jasper Campagna
San Mateo, CA

Capt. Kookaburra

1 oz. Captain Morgan Original spiced rum
3/4 oz. Baileys Irish Cream (float)

Captain's Cannonball

1 part Captain Morgan Original spiced rum
2 parts orange juice
1 part cranberry juice

The House of Seagram
New York, NY

Captain's Hook

1 part Captain Morgan Original spiced rum
1 part Captain Morgan Parrot Bay rum
1 part orange juice
1 part pineapple juice
splash cranberry juice

Barry Collins
Buffalo, NY

Caramel Apple

Schoenauer Apfel schnapps

Put one caramel candy in a shot glass and fill with Schoenauer Apfel schnapps. Shoot and chew candy!

Caribbean Cruise Shooter

1/3 shot Kahlúa
1/3 shot Baileys Irish Cream
1/3 shot CocoRibe

Build.

Caribbean Quartet

1 part Bacardi light rum
1 part Myers's Original dark rum
1 part Captain Morgan spiced rum
2 parts Midori melon liqueur
3 parts pineapple juice
splash grenadine

Shake with ice and strain.

Keith Myers, Italian Bistro
Newark, DE

Carrot Cake Shooter

1 oz. DeKuyper Buttershot schnapps
1/2 oz. DeKuyper Hot Damn cinnamon
  schnapps
1 1/2 oz. Baileys Irish Cream

Justin Cracchiola
Johnson City, TN

Cat Nip

1/2 oz. Sour Puss raspberry liqueur
1/4 oz. Stolichnaya vodka
1/4 oz. cranberry juice
splash soda

Tracey Waite
Grand Island, NE

Cement Mixer

3/4 oz. Baileys Irish Cream
3/4 oz. Rose's lime juice

Build.

Chadallac

1/3 Jagermeister
1/3 Llord's amaretto
1/3 Malibu rum
pineapple juice

Chad Plumley
Huntington, WV

Chambeird

1/2 oz. Chambord
1/2 oz. vodka
1/4 oz. orange juice
1/4 oz. pineapple juice

Shake with ice and strain.

Chambord & Wild Spirit

1/2 oz. Wild Spirit
1/2 oz. Chambord

Shake with ice and strain.

Chambord Iceberg

4 parts Chambord
1 part Absolut vodka

Shake with ice and strain.

Champagne Royal

1/4 oz. Chambord
1 3/4 oz. champagne

Build.

Charlie Chaplin

1 oz. sloe gin
1 oz. apricot-flavored brandy
1 oz. lemon juice

Shake with ice and strain into cordial glass.

Charlie's Angel

3/4 oz. amaretto
1/4 oz. cream

Shake with ice and strain.

Cheerleader

1 oz. Disaronno amaretto
1/2 oz. cranberry juice
dash Rose's lime juice

Shake with ice and strain.

Cheesecake

1 oz. blueberry schnapps
1/2 oz. Kahlúa
1 1/2 oz. cream

Shake with ice and strain.

Cherry Bomb

1/2 oz. Kahlúa
1/2 oz. crème de banana
1/4 oz. Myers's rum cream
1/4 oz. cherry brandy

Cherry Bomb #2

1 oz. cherry brandy
1/3 oz. Bacardi 151 rum

Build.

Cherry Hooper

1/4 oz. cherry brandy
1 oz. orange juice

Build.

Cherry Lifesaver

3/4 oz. cherry brandy
1/4 oz. banana liqueur
1 oz. sweet & sour mix

Shake with ice and strain.

Chia Pet

tequila
Midori

Equal parts.

Ryan Peters
Liberty Corner, NJ

Chiclet

1 oz. Cuervo tequila
1/2 oz. triple sec
splash Rose's lime juice
splash sweet & sour mix

Baja Cantina
Park City, UT

Chilled Kurant

Absolut Kurant vodka

Use chilled Kurant with cherries rolled in sugar. Serve in shot glass.

China Beach

1 part Canton ginger liqueur
1/2 part vodka
2 parts cranberry juice

Build.

China White

1/3 oz. white crème de cacao
1/3 oz. Baileys Irish Cream
1/3 oz. Canton ginger liqueur

Chinese Torture

4 parts Canton ginger liqueur
1 part Bombay gin

Build.

Chinese Torture #2

1 part Canton ginger liqueur
1 part Bacardi 151 rum

Build.

Chip Shot

3/4 oz. Baileys Irish Cream
3/4 oz. Tuaca liqueur
splash coffee

Build.

Chip Shot #2

1/2 oz. Kahlúa
1/2 oz. Baileys Irish Cream
1/2 oz. cream

Chocolate Almond Pie

3/4 oz. Disaronno amaretto
3/4 oz. dark crème de cacao
1/2 oz. cream

Shake with ice and strain.

Chocolate Banana

1/2 oz. banana liqueur
1/2 oz. dark crème de cacao
1/2 oz. cream

Shake with ice and strain.

Chocolate Covered Cherry

1/2 oz. Kahlúa
1/2 oz. Baileys Irish Cream
1/3 oz. grenadine

Build.

Chocolate Covered Cherry #2

1 oz. Absolut Kurant vodka
1/2 oz. Kahlúa
1/2 oz. Baileys Irish Cream

Serve with a cherry in the bottom.

Chocolate Covered Cherry #3

2 parts Disaronno amaretto
2 parts Baileys Irish Cream
1 part grenadine

First put the grenadine on the bottom, then
layer amaretto and Baileys on top.

Chocolate Cream Peaches

1/2 oz. Kahlúa
1/2 oz. peach schnapps
1/2 oz. cream

Build.

Chocolate Kangaroo

1 oz. Tia Maria
1/2 oz. Hiram Walker dark crème de cacao
1/2 oz. cream

Shake with ice and strain.

Chocolate Milk

2 parts Mozart chocolate liqueur
3 parts cream

Shake with ice and strain.

Chocolate Milk Shake

1/2 oz. Licor 43
1/2 oz. dark crème de cacao
1/2 oz. milk

Shake with ice and strain.

Chocolate Monkey

1 1/2 oz. crème de banana
1/2 oz. dark crème de cacao
1/2 oz. cream

Shake with ice and strain.

Chocolate Mounds

1/2 oz. Malibu
1/2 oz. Kahlúa
1/2 oz. cream

Shake with ice and strain.

Chocolate Orgasm

1/2 oz. Mozart chocolate liqueur
1/2 oz. Disaronno amaretto
1/2 oz. Baileys Irish Cream
1/2 oz. cream (optional)

Shake with ice and strain.

Chocolate Pucker

1/2 oz. Absolut vodka
1/2 oz. crème de banana
1/2 oz. white crème de cacao
1/2 oz. lemonade

Shake with ice and strain.

Joe Carter
Charlie & Barney's Bar & Grill
Indianapolis, IN

Chocolate Raspberry

1 oz. Chambord
1/2 oz. Kahlúa
1/2 oz. cream

Shake with ice and strain.

Chocolate Rattlesnake Shooter

2/3 oz. Kahlúa
1/3 oz. white crème de cacao
2/3 oz. Baileys Irish Cream
1/3 oz. Rumple Minze peppermint schnapps

Build.

Choc-O-Mint

1 part Rumple Minze peppermint schnapps
1 part Godiva chocolate liqueur

Chill over ice and strain.

Georgie Atfield
The Library Bar & Restaurant
Woodcliff Lake, NJ

Chopper Stopper

1/2 oz. Absolut vodka
1/2 oz. Bacardi rum
splash Midori
3 oz. strawberry Holland House mix
1 oz. piña colada mix
splash pineapple juice

Served frozen, not solid.

K.W. Chamberlain
Andover, MA

Christmas Mist

1 oz. triple sec
1/2 oz. Rumple Minze peppermint schnapps

Shake with ice and strain.

Cincinnati Bengals

1/2 Black Haus blackberry schnapps
1/2 Stolichnaya Ohranj vodka

Marybeth & Beck Hill
West Chester, OH

Cinnamon Mold

1 1/2 oz. cinnamon schnapps
1/2 oz. cream

Shake with ice and strain.

Circus Peanut

1/2 oz. crème de banana
1/2 oz. vodka
whipped cream
splash grenadine

Chill, shake, and serve.

Dave Warren
Billy Froggs' Grill and Bar
Omaha, NE

Citron My Face

1 part Absolut Citron
1 part Key Largo schnapps
1 part sour mix
1 part cranberry juice
1 part pineapple juice

Mark J. Sheehan
Fairfax, VA

Citrus Shooter

3/2 oz. Absolut vodka
3/4 oz. triple sec
1/2 splash orange juice
1/2 splash cranberry juice
1/2 splash pineapple juice

Shake with ice and strain.

Clay Pigeon

1 oz. vodka
1 oz. apple juice

Clementine

3/4 oz. Absolut Mandarin
1 oz. cranberry juice
1/2 oz. sweet & sour mix

Pour all three ingredients into a shaker with ice. Must stir! Strain and pour into a shot glass.

Stephanie S. Russell
Vero Beach, FL

Cloud 9

1 oz. Metaxa ouzo
1/2 oz. blueberry schnapps

Build.

Cloud Nine

1 oz. ouzo
1/2 oz. blueberry schnapps

Layer in shot glass.

Wendel Bryant
El Campo, TX

Cloudy Day

1/4 oz. Malibu
1/4 oz. Chambord
1/4 oz. Midori melon liqueur
1 oz. pineapple juice
dash cream

Shake with ice and strain.

Coco Loco Shot

1 oz. tequila
1 oz. CoCo Lopéz cream of coconut

Axel Berenes
San Jose, CA

Coconut Bon-Bon

1/2 oz. coconut rum
1/4 oz. Disaronno amaretto
1/4 oz. dark crème de cacao
1/4 oz. orange juice
1/4 oz. cream

Shake with ice and strain.

Coffee Bean

3/4 oz. Kahlúa
3/4 oz. anisette
1/4 oz. Southern Comfort

Build.

Cold Gold

1 1/2 parts Der Lachs Original
   Goldwasser, chilled

Serve with your favorite beer on the side.

Colorado M.F.

1/2 oz. Absolut vodka
1/4 oz. Bacardi 151 rum
1/2 oz. Kahlúa
1/2 oz. cream

Shake with ice and strain. Dash of soda.

Coma

1/3 oz. Kahlúa
1/3 oz. crème de banana
1/3 oz. anisette

Comfort Zone

1/2 oz. Southern Comfort
1/2 oz. Disaronno amaretto
1/2 oz. pineapple juice

Shake with ice and strain.

Comfortable Woo

1/2 oz. Absolut vodka
1/2 oz. peach schnapps
1/2 oz. Southern Comfort
1/2 oz. cranberry juice

Chill and strain.

Lori Stewart
Friends Lounge
Lowell, MA

Cool Citron

1 oz. Absolut Citron vodka
1/2 oz. Hiram Walker white crème de
  menthe

Build.

Cool Mint Listerine

1/3 oz. vodka
1/3 oz. peppermint schnapps
1/3 oz. blue curacao

Flin Brian
Kamloops
British Columbia, Canada

Cool Peppar

1 1/4 oz. Absolut Peppar
wedge of lime

Pour freezer-cold Absolut Peppar into a shot glass. Squeeze the juice of lime wedge into the glass.

Cool-Aid

1/2 oz. Disaronno amaretto
1/2 oz. Midori melon liqueur
1 oz. cranberry juice

Shake with ice and strain. Top with soda.

Cool-Aid #2

1/3 oz. Midori melon liqueur
1/3 oz. Disaronno amaretto
1/3 oz. pineapple juice

Build.

Cool-Aid #3

1/3 oz. Southern Comfort
1/3 oz. Disaronno amaretto
1/3 oz. cranberry juice

Build.

Cordless Screwdriver

1 3/4 oz. Absolut vodka
orange wedge
sugar

Chill vodka and strain into shot glass. Dip orange wedge in sugar. Shoot the vodka, and bite the orange.

Cosmic Aphrodisiac

1/2 oz. Bacardi Limón
1/2 oz. peach schnapps
1/2 oz. strawberry schnapps
splash sour mix

Frend Gondermann
Palatine, IL

Cosmic Milk

1 oz. Tequila Rose
1/2 oz. amaretto
1/2 oz. banana liqueur

Goran Perovic
Akron, OH

Cosmos

1 1/2 oz. Finlandia vodka
1/2 oz. lime juice

Shake with ice and strain.

Cough Drop

1 1/4 oz. blackberry brandy
1 1/4 oz. Rumple Minze peppermint
  schnapps

Build.

Cough Drop #2

3/4 oz. Chambord
3/4 oz. Rumple Minze peppermint schnapps

Build.

Cowboy

1 1/2 oz. whiskey
1/2 oz. cream

Shake with ice and strain.

Cran-A-Kazi

1 1/2 oz. vodka
1/4 oz. triple sec
1/4 oz. Rose's lime juice
1/4 oz. cranberry juice

Shake with ice and strain.

Cran-Apple

1 oz. apple schnapps
1 oz. cranberry juice

Shake with ice and strain.

Cream of Beef

1 1/4 oz. Carolans Irish Cream
1/2 oz. Beefeater gin

Build.

Cream Soda

3/4 oz. Captain Morgan spiced rum
1/2 oz. ginger ale

Build.

Creamsicle

1/2 oz. Cointreau
1/2 oz. Liquore Galliano
1 oz. cream

Shake with ice and strain.

Creamsicle #2

3/4 oz. Licor 43
1/4 oz. white crème de cacao
1/2 oz. orange juice
1/4 oz. cream

Shake with ice and strain.

Creamy Orgasm

1/2 oz. vodka
1/2 oz. Kahlúa
1/2 oz. Disaronno amaretto
1/2 oz. cream

Shake with ice and strain.

Creamy Saintsation

3/4 oz. Baileys Irish Cream
3/4 oz. Maui tropical schnapps
3/4 oz. DeKuyper Mad Melon watermelon
   schnapps

Harvey Shiran
San Antonio, TX

Creature from the Black Lagoon

1 part Jagermeister
1 part Romana black sambuca

Shake with ice and strain.

Cripple Creek

1/2 oz. Old Grand Dad bourbon
1/2 oz. tequila
1/4 oz. Liquore Galliano
1 oz. orange juice

Shake with ice and strain. Float Galliano.

Crispy Shooter

1/2 oz. Kahlúa
1/2 oz. Disaronno amaretto
1/2 oz. Rumple Minze peppermint schnapps

Shake with ice and strain.

Cross-Eyed Mary

3/4 oz. Beefeater gin
3/4 oz. Bacardi Limón
splash cola

Shake with ice; strain into shot glass.

Bonnie S. Bailey
Wappingers Falls, NY

Cruise Missile

1/4 oz. vodka
1/2 oz. blue curacao
1/2 oz. crème de noyaux
1/4 oz. grapefruit juice

Shake with ice and strain.

Cuervo Popper

1 oz. Jose Cuervo Gold tequila
1/4 oz. ginger ale

Build.

Curly Cue

1 part Baileys Irish Cream
1 part Goldschlager cinnamon schnapps

Shake with ice and strain.

Mary Gibbeson
Deer Lodge
Ojai, CA

Dallas Alice

Grand Marnier
tequila
amaretto

Equal parts. Shake with ice and strain.

Darlington's Delight

green crème de menthe
Godet belgian white chocolate liqueur

Pour crème de menthe in shot glass. Layer
Godet liqueur on top.

Jim Darlington
Astor, PA

Day in the Shade

1 oz. Hiram Walker CocoRhum
1/2 oz. cranberry juice
1/2 oz. pineapple juice

Shake with ice and strain.

DC-3

1/3 oz. Kahlúa
1/2 oz. anisette
1/3 oz. Baileys Irish Cream

Dead Canary

1 oz. Finlandia vodka
1/4 oz. Grand Marnier
1/4 oz. pineapple juice

Shake with ice and strain.

Dead Doctor

Dr. McGillicuddy's peppermint schnapps
Kahlúa
Jagermeister

Equal parts. Serve chilled in shot glass.
Build.

Cindy Smith
Bob Smith's Sports Club
Hudson, WI

Dead Rat

1 oz. Usquaebach scotch
1/3 oz. Chartreuse

Shake with ice and strain.

Deep Throat

1/2 oz. Kahlúa
1/2 oz. Fris vodka

Top with whipped cream.

Dennis the Menace

1 oz. Malibu
1/2 oz. peach schnapps
splash cranberry juice

Shake with ice and strain.

Depth Charge

Mug beer
1 oz. Rumple Minze peppermint schnapps

Drop shot glass in beer and down.

Desert Sunrise

1 oz. DeKuyper cactus juice liqueur
splash Rose's lime juice

Serve chilled.

Designer Jeans

1/2 oz. Baileys Irish Cream
1/2 oz. Chambord
1/2 oz. Myers's Original dark rum

Shake with ice and strain.

Devil's Blood

1 1/4 oz. tequila
splash Tabasco
3/4 oz. tomato juice

Shake with ice and strain.

Dirty Adrian

1/2 oz. Dr. McGillicuddy's vanilla schnapps
1/2 oz. Baileys Irish Cream
1/2 oz. Godiva

James Byrne
Oswego, NY

Dirty Devil

3/4 oz. vodka
1/2 oz. Kahlúa
1/2 oz. Liquore Galliano
dash Bacardi 151 rum

Layer in order. Place lime wheel over shot glass, sprinkle with sugar. Float 151 on wheel.

Dirty Harry

1 oz. Grand Marnier
1 oz. Tia Maria

Shake with ice and strain.

Dirty Peach

3/4 oz. peach schnapps
1/2 oz. Kahlúa
1/2 oz. cream
dash pineapple juice

Shake with ice and strain.

Dog Breath

1 1/2 oz. Fernet Branca
Red Dog beer

Shoot Fernet Branca with Red Dog on the side.

Dollar Bill

1 oz. Frïs vodka
3/4 oz. Midori melon liqueur
1/8 oz. Rose's lime juice

Shake with ice and strain.

Don Q Cristal Kiss

1 1/2 oz. Don Q Cristal rum
1/2 oz. blue curacao
4 oz. Tropicana orange juice

Shake with ice, strain, and pour.

Double Jack

1/2 oz. Yukon Jack
1/2 oz. Jack Daniel's

Shake with ice and strain.

Double Vision

1 oz. Tia Maria
1/4 oz. Romana sambuca
1/4 oz. brandy

Shake with ice and strain.

Doublemint

1 part Hiram Walker peppermint schnapps
1 part Hiram Walker spearmint schnapps

Build.

Dr. Pepper

1 part Disaronno amaretto
1 part root beer schnapps
1/2 glass beer

Fill shot glass with amaretto and root beer schnapps. Drop shot glass into beer.

Drambuie Dragon

2 oz. Drambuie
6 drops Tabasco

Coat shot glass with 6 drops of Tabasco, fill with Drambuie, and serve straight up.

Dream Shake

1 oz. Baileys Irish Cream
1/2 oz. Tia Maria

Shake with ice and strain.

Dreamsicle

1 1/4 oz. amaretto
1/2 oz. orange juice
1/2 oz. cream

Shake with ice and strain.

Drunk Irish Monk

1 1/4 oz. Carolans Irish Cream
3/4 oz. Hiram Walker hazelnut liqueur

Shake with ice and strain.

Drunk Monk

3/4 oz. Hiram Walker hazelnut liqueur
1 1/4 oz. Bacardi rum

Shake with ice and strain.

Duck Fart

3/4 oz. Kahlúa
3/4 oz. Carolans Irish Cream
1/2 oz. Canadian Club whiskey

Build.

Duck Pin

3/4 oz. Chambord
3/4 oz. Stolichnaya vodka
1/2 oz. pineapple juice

Shake with ice and strain.

Duck Pin #2

1 oz. Chambord
1/2 oz. Southern Comfort
1/2 oz. pineapple juice

Shake with ice and strain.

Dunham Good

1 oz. Goldschlager cinnamon schnapps
1/2 oz. Disaronno amaretto

Shake with ice and strain.

Dunikaze

amaretto
Rumple Minze peppermint schnapps
blackberry brandy
float Jim Beam bourbon

Equal parts.

Dusty Rose

1 oz. Chambord
1 oz. Baileys Irish Cream

Shake with ice and strain.

E.K. Up

2 parts Echte Kroatzbeere blackberry
  liqueur

Serve straight up, well chilled.

E.T.

1/3 oz. Midori melon liqueur
1/2 oz. Baileys Irish Cream
1/3 oz. Absolut vodka

Build.

Earthquake

3/4 oz. anisette
3/4 oz. Disaronno amaretto
1/4 oz. Southern Comfort

Build.

Earthquake #2

Equal parts:
   Disaronno amaretto
   Aftershock

Lynn Kirsch
Winter Park, FL

Easter Egg

1/2 oz. Chambord
1/2 oz. Tia Maria
1/2 oz. cream

Build.

Ejaculation

1/2 oz. white crème de cacao
1/2 oz. white crème de menthe
1/2 oz. Baileys Irish Cream
3/4 oz. vodka

Ramsey Luke
Beverly Hills, CA

El Chico

1 oz. tequila
1/2 oz. triple sec
1/2 oz. Rose's lime juice
2 dashes Angostura bitters

Shake with ice and strain.

El Torito

1 oz. Sauza Conmemorativo tequila
1/2 oz. Hiram Walker dark crème de cacao

Build.

Electric Banana

1/2 oz. tequila
1/2 oz. crème de banana

Electric Popsicle

1/2 oz. Chambord
1/2 oz. vodka
1/2 oz. crème de banana
1/2 oz. lime juice

Electric Sambuca

1 shot sambuca
1 shot blue curacao

Don Voight
Willow Springs, IL

Elephant's Foot

1 part Kahlúa
1 part Stolichnaya vodka
1 part Grand Marnier
1 part Licor 43
1 part cream

Shake with ice and strain.

Elwoods Shooter

dash crème de cassis
1 oz. pineapple juice
3/4 oz. amaretto

Shake with ice and strain.

Empire Strikes Back

1/4 oz. Smirnoff 100 proof vodka
1/4 oz. Southern Comfort
1/4 oz. Grand Marnier
1/4 oz. Disaronno amaretto
1/4 oz. pineapple juice

Shake with ice and strain.

Energizer

1/2 oz. Benedictine
1/2 oz. Baileys Irish Cream
1/2 oz. Grand Marnier

Build.

Erin Cross

3/4 oz. Celtic Crossing Irish liqueur
3/4 oz. Baileys Irish Cream
1/2 oz. Black Bush Irish whiskey

Mike Byers
Fife, WA

Eskimo Slugger

1 part Rumple Minze
1 part Baileys Irish Cream
1 part California butterscotch schnapps

Craig Hayen
Brookings, SD

Evening Shade

3/4 oz. Baileys Irish Cream
3/4 oz. buttershots schnapps
splash pineapple juice

Pam Payton
St. Roberts, MO

Eye Drop

1/2 oz. Rumple Minze peppermint schnapps
1/2 oz. Metaxa Ouzo
1/2 oz. Stolichnaya vodka

Build.

Eye to Eye (I to I)

1 oz. Carolans Irish Cream
1 oz. Tullamore Dew Irish whiskey

Shake with ice and strain.

F-16

1/3 Kahlúa
1/3 Baileys Irish Cream
1/3 brandy

Build.

F-16 #2

1/3 Kahlúa
1/3 Baileys Irish Cream
1/3 Bacardi 151 rum

Build.

F-16 #3

1/2 oz. Carolans Irish Cream
1/2 oz. Hiram Walker hazelnut liqueur
1/2 oz. Kahlúa

Shake with ice and strain.

F-52

Kahlúa
Baileys Irish Cream
Frangelico

Equal parts. Build.

Fanny Pack

1 oz. Finlandia vodka
1/2 oz. Finlandia cranberry vodka
2 oz. orange juice
1/4 oz. pineapple juice

Shake with ice and strain.

Fender Bender

peach schnapps
Green Chartreuse

Equal parts. Build.

Fifth Avenue

1/2 oz. dark crème de cacao
1/2 oz. apricot-flavored brandy
1 tbsp. light cream

Layer in order in cordial glass.

Fifty-Fifty (50-50) Bar

1 oz. Baileys Irish Cream
1 oz. Kahlúa
splash Bacardi 151 rum

Float Bacardi, serve.

Fifty-Seven ('57) T-Bird

1/2 oz. Southern Comfort
1/2 oz. Grand Marnier
1/2 oz. Disaronno amaretto
1/2 oz. pineapple juice

Shake with ice and strain.

Fifty-Seven ('57) T-Bird with Detroit Plates

1 part vodka
1 part Grand Marnier
1 part amaretto
1 part Southern Comfort
1 part pineapple juice

Shake with ice and strain.

Fifty-Seven ('57) T-Bird with Texas Plates

Myers's Original dark rum
sloe gin
Grand Marnier
grapefruit juice

Equal parts. Shake with ice and strain.

Finger Wiggle

1/4 oz. Crantasia schnapps
1/2 oz. Malibu rum
splash Absolut Citron
splash cranberry juice
splash sour mix

Christine "CK" Kotila
Warren, MI

Finnigan's Wake

1 oz. Finlandia vodka
1/4 oz. melon liqueur
1/2 oz. pineapple juice

Mix as a shot.

Fire & Ice

3/4 oz. Rumple Minze peppermint schnapps
3/4 oz. Bacardi 151 rum

Build.

Fire Bomb

3/4 oz. Fris vodka
3/4 oz. Hiram Walker Red Hot schnapps
dash Tabasco
dash cayenne pepper

Shake with ice and strain.

Fire Breathing Dragon

1 part Bacardi 151 rum
1 part Goldschlager cinnamon schnapps
2 drops Tabasco

Rory L. Chatman
Norfolk, VA

Fireball

1 oz. Dr. McGillicuddy's peppermint
   schnapps
1 oz. cherry brandy

Shake with ice and strain.

Fireball #2

1 oz. cinnamon schnapps
1/2 oz. vodka
1/2 oz. grenadine

Shake with ice and strain.

Fireball #3

1 1/2 oz. cinnamon schnapps
dash Tabasco

Shake with ice and strain.

Firecracker

1 part blue curacao
1 part Baileys Irish Cream
1 part sloe gin

In a shooter glass float first two ingredients
to form layers. Pour sloe gin lightly on top.

Alice Whitmer
Pelles Sports Bar
Fair Haven, MI

Firecracker #2

3/4 oz. Rumple Minze peppermint schnapps
drop Tabasco
dash grenadine
dash soda

Dribble in dash of grenadine, dash of soda.

121

Firewater

1 part Rumple Minze peppermint schnapps
1 part cinnamon schnapps
3 drops Bacardi 151 rum

Build.

Flame Thrower

1/3 oz. white crème de cacao
1/3 oz. Benedictine
1/3 oz. brandy

Flaming Shorts

1/3 oz. Kahlúa
1/3 oz. Baileys Irish Cream
1/3 oz. Green Chartreuse

Build.

Floaters Shooter

2/3 shot Black Velvet Canadian whiskey
1 oz. orange juice

Float Black Velvet.

Florida Joy
1 1/4 oz. Absolut Citron vodka
1/2 oz. Grand Marnier

Mix with cracked ice in a shaker or blender
and pour into shot glass.

Flying Banana
1/2 oz. crème de banana
1/2 oz. Parrot Bay rum
orange juice
splash grenadine

Flying Grasshopper
1/2 oz. green crème de menthe
1/2 oz. white crème de cacao
1/2 oz. Smirnoff vodka

Stir with ice and strain in cordial glass.

Flying Purple People Eater

1 part blue curacao
1 part DeKuyper Wildberry schnapps
1 part Absolut vodka
cranberry juice

Fill with cranberry juice. Build.

Jennifer Lisa Weir
American Athletic Club Café
Milford, MA

Fog

1 oz. Stolichnaya vodka
1/2 oz. cranberry juice
juice of fresh lime

Shake with ice and strain.

Foghorn

3/4 oz. Bombay gin
3/4 oz. ginger ale
dash Rose's lime juice

Shake with ice and strain.

Fools Gold

1 part Finlandia vodka
1 part Liquore Galliano

Build.

Forbidden Cinnamon Apple

1/2 oz. Leroux apple schnapps
1/4 oz. Goldschlager cinnamon schnapps
1/4 oz. Absolut vodka

Chill over ice and strain into shooter glass.

Georgie Atfield
The Library Bar & Restaurant
Woodcliff Lake, NJ

Fortified

2 parts DeKuyper cactus juice
1 part Jose Cuervo Especial tequila

Donna Luther
Ketchikan, AK

Fourth of July

3/4 oz. Rumple Minze peppermint
   schnapps
3/4 oz. blue curacao
splash grenadine

Build.

Foxy Lady

1 oz. Disaronno amaretto
1/2 oz. Stolichnaya vodka
1 oz. blue curacao

Layer in order in cordial glass.

Freddy Kruger

1/4 oz. Romana sambuca
1/4 oz. Jagermeister
3/4 oz. vodka

Build.

French Choo Choo

1 oz. Southern Comfort
1 oz. Grand Marnier

Shake with ice and strain.

French Connection

1 part Courvoisier
1 part Grand Marnier

Shake with ice and strain.

French Hooker

3/4 oz. Absolut vodka
3/4 oz. Chambord
1 splash sour mix

Stir and strain.

French Kamikaze

3/4 oz. vodka
1/2 oz. Chambord
dash Rose's lime juice

Shake with ice and strain.

French Kiss

1 part Martini & Rossi sweet vermouth
1 part Martini & Rossi dry vermouth

Build.

127

French Tickler

2/3 oz. Goldschlager cinnamon schnapps
1/2 oz. Grand Marnier

Shake with ice and strain.

French Toast

1 oz. cinnamon schnapps
1 oz. club soda

Build.

Früs Your Nuts

1/2 oz. Früs vodka
1/2 oz. Hiram Walker hazelnut liqueur

Shake with ice and strain.

Frog in a Blender

splash Jagermeister
2 parts Baileys Irish Cream
1 part green crème de menthe

Add crème de menthe drop by drop. Rim
shooter glass with grenadine and sugar. It
should look like a blended frog.

Max Burnett
Studio City, CA

Fru-Fru

banana liqueur
peach schnapps
pineapple juice
splash lime juice

Equal amounts. Build.

Fruit & Nuts

3/4 oz. Chambord
3/4 oz. Frangelico
1/2 oz. cranberry juice
1/4 oz. cream

Amy Jane Louise
Hoboken, NJ

Fruit Lifesaver

3/4 oz. Hiram Walker crème de banana
3/4 oz. Hiram Walker blackberry brandy

Build.

Full Moon

3/4 oz. Grand Marnier
3/4 oz. Hiram Walker amaretto liqueur

Build.

Funky Bitch

1/2 oz. Kahlúa
1/2 oz. vodka
1/4 oz. Baileys Irish Cream
1/4 oz. Frangelico

Shake with ice and strain.

Funky Monkey

1/4 oz. Baileys Irish Cream
1/4 oz. crème de banana
1/4 oz. butterscotch schnapps
1/4 oz. half & half

Steve Cochran
Irvine, CA

Fuzzy Antler

3/4 oz. Canadian Mist
3/4 oz. peach schnapps

Shake with ice and strain.

Fuzzy Melon

1 oz. Midori melon liqueur
1 oz. Hiram Walker peach schnapps
splash cream
splash orange juice
splash pineapple juice

Shake with ice and strain.

Fuzzy Mexican

1 oz. Cuervo 1800 tequila
splash DeKuyper Peachtree schnapps

Robert Turlington
Brockport, NY

Fuzzy Navel

1 part DeKuyper Peachtree schnapps
2 parts orange juice

Build.

Fuzzy Pirate

1/2 oz. Captain Morgan spiced rum
1/2 oz. peach schnapps
1 oz. cranberry juice

Build.

G&C

1/3 oz. Liquore Galliano
2/3 oz. Remy Martin cognac

Float cognac on Galliano in 1 oz. pony glass.

G&G

1 oz. Liquore Galliano
1/2 oz. Candolini Grappa

Build.

Galactic Ale

1 oz. Frïs vodka
1 oz. blue curacao
1 oz. lime juice
1/2 oz. Chambord

Shake with ice and strain. Serves two.

Galliano Hot Shot

3/4 oz. Liquore Galliano
3/4 oz. hot coffee

Into a shooter glass, float one ingredient over another in above order to form layers. Top with whipped cream.

Galliano Viking

3/4 oz. Liquore Galliano
3/4 oz. vodka

Build.

Gallstone Shooter

3/4 oz. crème de noyaux
3/4 oz. white crème de cacao
1/2 oz. Absolut vodka

Shake and strain.

Gangrene

1/2 Jagermeister
1/2 Midori melon liqueur

Build.

Gargleblaster

1/2 oz. Midori melon liqueur
1 oz. Bacardi light rum
1/4 oz. Bacardi 151 rum

Build.

Garter Belt

1 1/4 oz. Bacardi Amber rum

Serve in shot glass.

Gator Juice

2 parts Crystal Comfort liqueur
1 part blue curacao
1 part orange juice
1 splash Rose's lime juice

Shake with ice and strain.

German Death

1/2 oz. Jagermeister
1/2 oz. Rumple Minze peppermint schnapps

Build.

German Milkshake

1 oz. Jagermeister
1 oz. dark crème de cacao
1 oz. cream

Shake with ice and strain.

Ghostbusters

3/4 oz. peach schnapps
3/4 oz. vodka
dash orange juice
dash cranberry juice
dash cream

Shake and strain.

Gin & Sin

1 1/2 oz. Beefeater gin
1/2 oz. sweet & sour mix
1/2 oz. orange juice
splash grenadine

Shake with ice and strain.

Ginger Snap

1 1/2 oz. Canton ginger liqueur
1/2 oz. sparkling water

Shoot or use as a popper.

Glow Work

3/4 oz. Old Grand Dad bourbon
3/4 oz. Midori melon liqueur
1/2 oz. pineapple juice

Shake and strain.

135

Godchild

3/4 oz. Disaronno amaretto
3/4 oz. brandy

Build.

Godfather

1/4 oz. Disaronno amaretto
1 1/4 oz. J&B Scotch

Build.

Godmother

1/2 oz. Disaronno amaretto
1 1/2 oz. Stolichnaya vodka

Build.

Gold Freeze

Keep bottle of Der Lachs Original Goldwasser in freezer; enjoy ice shots straight up.

Gold Furnace

1 oz. Goldschlager cinnamon schnapps
2 dashes Tabasco

Build.

Gold Rush

1/2 oz. Goldschlager cinnamon schnapps
1/2 oz. Cuervo Gold tequila

Build.

Gold Russian

1 part Goldschlager cinnamon schnapps
1 part Kahlúa

Shake with ice and strain.

Golden Apple

3/4 oz. Apple Barrel schnapps
1/4 oz. Goldschlager

Layer Goldschlager on top of the Apple Barrel schnapps.

Brett May
Hughesville, PA

Golden Cadillac

1/2 oz. white crème de cacao
1/2 oz. Liquore Galliano
1 oz. cream

Shake with ice and strain.

Golden Dragon

1 3/4 oz. brandy
1 tbsp. Yellow Chartreuse

Pour Chartreuse and float brandy on top.

Golden Dream

1/2 oz. Liquore Galliano
1/2 oz. triple sec
1/2 oz. orange juice
1/2 oz. cream

Shake with ice and strain.

Golden Gorilla

1/2 oz. Puerto Rican rum
1/2 oz. Hiram Walker crème de banana
1/2 oz. pineapple juice
1/2 oz. orange juice
1/4 oz. Liquore Galliano

Shake with ice and strain. Float Galliano.

Jack Howley
Tampa, FL

Golden Nipple

3/4 oz. Liquore Galliano
3/4 oz. Kahlúa
whipped cream

In a shooter glass pour Galliano, then carefully float Kahlúa to form a layer. Top with whipped cream.

Golden Spike

3/4 oz. Liquore Galliano
3/4 oz. Drambuie
1/4 oz. J&B scotch

Build.

Goldfinger

1 1/2 oz. Goldschlager cinnamon schnapps

Use ice-cold Goldschlager. Serve and lick the finger!

Goldschlager & Lager

1 1/2 oz. Goldschlager cinnamon schnapps
12 oz. beer

Shoot ice-cold Goldschlager with an ice-cold beer.

Good 'N Plenty

3/4 oz. Hiram Walker anisette
3/4 oz. Kahlúa

Shake with ice and strain.

Good 'N Plenty #2

1 oz. anisette
1 oz. blackberry brandy

Build.

Good 'N Plenty #3

1/4 oz. Frïs vodka
1/4 oz. Kahlúa
1/4 oz. Hiram Walker anisette
1/2 oz. cream

Shake with ice and strain.

Goodnight

1 part Avalanche
1 part Aftershock
1 part Goldschlager

Ryan Clark
Orlando, FL

Gorilla Fart Shooter

1 part Bacardi 151 rum
1 part Wild Turkey 101 bourbon

Build.

Graham Cracker

1/2 oz. Baileys Irish Cream
1/2 oz. butterscotch schnapps
1/2 oz. Goldschlager
1/2 oz. cream

Gran-Cran

1 oz. Finlandia cranberry vodka
1/4 oz. Grand Marnier

Build.

Grand Am

1 part Grand Marnier
1 part Disaronno amaretto

Build.

Grand Slam

1 part Grand Marnier
2 parts Tangueray gin
2 parts orange juice
1 splash grenadine

Shake with ice, pour into a test tube, and top it off with a cherry.

Grape Ape

1 part Absolut vodka
2 parts grape juice
1 part 7-Up

Build.

Grape Crush

1 oz. Smirnoff vodka
1/2 oz. Chambord
1/2 oz. sour mix

Shake with ice and strain. Top with 7-Up.

Grape Juice

1/2 oz. vodka
1/2 oz. blueberry schnapps
1/2 oz. Chambord
splash blue curacao
splash cranberry juice

Judi North
Margate, NJ

Grape Lax

1 oz. Chambord
1 oz. blue curacao
splash 7-Up
splash cranberry juice

Build.

Grape Nehi

1 3/4 oz. Absolut Kurant vodka
3/4 oz. cranberry juice
splash club soda

Shake with ice and strain. Top with club soda.

Grasshoper

1 part green crème de menthe
1 part white crème de cacao
1 part vodka
2 parts cream or milk

Shake with ice and strain.

Greek Fire

1 oz. brandy
1/2 oz. Metaxa ouzo

Build.

Greek Revolution

1/2 oz. Liquore Galliano
1/2 oz. Metaxa ouzo
1/2 oz. grenadine

Into a shooter glass, pour grenadine. Carefully float ouzo, then Galliano to form 3 layers. Do not stir.

Green Apple

1/2 oz. apple schnapps
1/2 oz. Midori melon liqueur
1/4 oz. sour mix
dash 7-Up

Shake with ice and strain. Top with 7-Up.

Green Bullet

3/4 oz. green crème de menthe
3/4 oz. white crème de menthe
1/2 oz. Bacardi 151 rum

Shake with ice and strain.

Green Demon

1/2 oz. Smirnoff vodka
1/2 oz. Bacardi rum
1/2 oz. Midori melon liqueur
1/2 oz. lemonade

Shake with ice and strain.

Green Devil

1 1/2 oz. Beefeater gin
1/4 oz. Hiram Walker green crème de
  menthe
splash Rose's lime juice

Shake with ice and strain.

Green Dragon

1 oz. Green Chartreuse
1/2 oz. Bacardi 151 rum

Build.

Green Genie

1 oz. tequila
splash Tabasco
1 oz. Hiram Walker Green Chartreuse

Shake with ice and strain.

Green Hornet

3/4 oz. Southern Comfort
3/4 oz. green crème de menthe

Shake with ice and strain.

Green Lantern

3/4 oz. Green Chartreuse liqueur
3/4 oz. vodka
1/2 oz. triple sec

Shake with ice and strain.

Green Lizard

1 part Green Chartreuse
1 part Bacardi 151 rum
1 splash lime juice

Shake with ice and strain.

Green Meanie

3/4 oz. Southern Comfort
3/4 oz. Midori melon liqueur
1 splash pineapple juice

Shake with ice and strain.

Green Slime

1 part Bacardi rum
1 part Smirnoff vodka
1 part Midori melon liqueur
1 part orange juice
1 part pineapple juice

Blend and strain.
"If you can't do the time, don't drink the slime."

Tiny, Dr. of Mixology
McB's Pub
Skokie, IL

Green Sneaker

1/2 oz. Midori melon liqueur
1/2 oz. Hiram Walker triple sec
1 oz. Frïs vodka
2 oz. orange juice

Shake with ice and strain.

Green Spider

1 oz. white crème de cacao
1 oz. dark crème de menthe

Shake with ice and strain.

148

Green Weenie

Cuervo Gold tequila
Midori melon liqueur
sweet & sour mix

Equal parts. Build.

Pat Ensten
Brannigans Bar and Grill
Stillwater, OK

Greg's Warm Apple Pie Shooter

1/2 oz. Apple Barrel schnapps
1/2 oz. Berentzen liqueur
1/4 oz. butterscotch schnapps

Greg Musantry
Barnegat, NJ

Gremlin

1/4 oz. blue curacao
1/4 oz. Bacardi rum
1 oz. Absolut vodka
1/4 oz. orange juice

Shake with ice and strain.

G-Spot

1/2 oz. Midori
1/2 oz. amaretto
1/4 oz. triple sec
splash sweet & sour mix
splash pineapple juice

Corey Melendrez
Las Vegas, NV

Guillotine

3/4 oz. Smirnoff vodka
1/2 oz. Sauza tequila
1/2 oz. Rumble Minze peppermint schnapps

Shake with ice and strain.

Gum Drop

1 1/2 oz. Liquore Galliano
1 oz. Disaronno amaretto
1 oz. Licor 43
3 oz. pineapple juice
splash grenadine

Shake with ice and strain. Serves two.

Steven Cotsoradis, Jr.
Garden Bar
Baltimore, MD

Gumby

1/2 oz. Midori melon liqueur
1 1/4 oz. Frïs vodka
1/4 oz. 7-Up

Shake with ice and strain. Top with 7-Up.

Hairy Navel

1 part Absolut vodka
1 part DeKuyper Peachtree schnapps
2 parts orange juice

Build.

Half and Half

1/2 part Schoenauer Apfel schnapps
1/2 part Fuerst Bismarck

Use chilled Schoenauer Apfel schnapps and
Fuerst Bismarck. Pour into a shot glass.

Halloween Shooter

3/4 oz. Licor 43
3/4 oz. Opal Nera dark sambuca

Build.

Happy Camper

Equal parts:
  DeKuyper sour apple schnapps
  DeKuyper peach schnapps
  Absolut Citron vodka
splash orange juice
splash 7-Up

Carolyn Lemice
Las Vegas, NV

Happy Jack

1 1/2 oz. Jack Daniel's whiskey
1/2 oz. apple schnapps

Shake with ice and strain.

Harbor Lights

1 part Liquore Galliano
1 part Remy Martin

Build.

Harbor Lights #2

3/4 oz. Liquore Galliano
1/4 oz. Metaxa

Build.

Harbor Lights #3

3/4 oz. Chambord
3/4 oz. rum
1/2 oz. orange juice

Shake with ice and strain.

Harbor Lights #4

1/2 oz. amaretto
1/2 oz. Caffe Lolito liqueur
1/2 oz. Southern Comfort
1/2 oz. Bacardi 151 rum

Build.

Harbor Lights #5

1/2 oz. green crème de menthe
1/2 oz. Jack Daniel's black whiskey
1/2 oz. grenadine

Build.

Harbor Mist

1/2 oz. Myers's Original dark rum
1/2 oz. Tia Maria
1/2 oz. orange juice
1/2 oz. pineapple juice

Shake with ice and strain.

Harvey's Hot Shot

3/4 oz. Liquore Galliano
3/4 oz. orange juice
whipped cream

Pour Galliano and orange juice into a shaker. Pour unstrained into shot glass and top with whipped cream.

Hawaiian Punch

1/2 oz. Southern Comfort
1/2 oz. amaretto
1/2 oz. orange juice
1/2 oz. pineapple juice
dash grenadine

Add grenadine to color. Shake with ice and strain.

Hawaiian Punch #2

1/2 oz. crème de almond
1/2 oz. Southern Comfort
1/4 oz. Smirnoff 100 proof vodka
1/4 oz. pineapple juice

Shake with ice and strain.

Hawaiian Punch #3

3/4 oz. Southern Comfort
1/4 oz. Hiram Walker sloe gin
1/4 oz. Cointreau
1/2 oz. orange juice

Shake with ice and strain.

Head

3/4 oz. Hiram Walker root beer schnapps
3/4 oz. half & half

Layer.

Head Room

1/4 oz. Hiram Walker crème de banana
1/4 oz. Midori melon liqueur
1/2 oz. Carolans Irish Cream

Build.

Head Rush

1 part Chambord
1 part pear schnapps
1 part peach schnapps
1 part Romana sambuca
1 part Liquore Galliano
1 part Baileys Irish Cream

Baileys will automatically float itself. Serve in shot glass. Build.

David Willett, Days Inn
Fireside Lounge
So. Portland, ME

Heather's Hot Flash

1/2 oz. Absolut vodka
1/2 oz. Kahlúa
1/2 oz. buttershot schnapps
float Baileys Irish Cream

Heather Howie
Easton, PA

Heavy Metal

1 part Goldschlager cinnamon schnapps,
   chilled
1 part Jagermeister, chilled

Build.

Dan Culligan
Fort Collins Country Club
Fort Collins, CO

Hide the Banana

1/2 oz. Hiram Walker amaretto
1/2 oz. Midori melon liqueur
1/2 oz. Frïs vodka

Shake with ice and strain.

High Jamaican Wind

1 oz. Myers's Original dark rum
1/3 oz. Kahlúa
float half & half

Build.

157

Hit and Run

1 oz. Bombay gin
1 oz. anisette

Build.

Hollywood

3/4 oz. Chambord
3/4 oz. Finlandia vodka
1/2 oz. pineapple juice

Shake with ice and strain.

Honeysuckle Shooter

1 oz. Bacardi light rum
1 splash simple syrup
1/2 splash sour mix

Shake with ice and strain.

Hooter

1/2 oz. Hiram Walker amaretto
1/2 oz. Fris vodka
1/2 oz. grenadine
1/2 oz. orange juice

Shake with ice and strain.

Horny Lil' Indian

3/4 oz. Absolut vodka
1/4 oz. grenadine
1/4 oz. triple sec
splash tequila
1/4 oz. orange juice

Shake with ice and strain.

Rory L. Chatman
Norfolk, VA

Horny Monkey

1/4 oz. Kahlúa
1/4 oz. green crème de menthe
1/4 oz. crème de banana
1/4 oz. Baileys Irish Cream

Horny Wally

1/2 oz. Bacardi rum
1/2 oz. Midori
1 1/2 oz. curacao
splash sour mix
splash 7-Up

Greg Cohen
Rockville, MD

Hot Beach Shooter

3/4 oz. Malibu
3/4 oz. peach schnapps
1 oz. coffee

Build.

Hot Cherry Pie

1 oz. amaretto
1/2 oz. cranberry juice

Shake with ice and strain.

Hot Deck Shooter

1 oz. Crown Royal
2/3 oz. sweet vermouth
1 dash ginger

Shake with ice and strain.

Hot Goose

1 1/2 oz. Grand Marnier
1/2 oz. hot water

Shake and strain.

Hot Lava

1 1/4 oz. Absolut Peppar vodka
1/4 oz. Disaronno amaretto

Build.

Hot Monkey Love

1/3 oz. crème de banana
1/3 oz. Baileys Irish Cream
1/3 oz. Original Bartenders Hot Sex

Adam Powell
Madison, WI

Hot Nuts

1 1/2 oz. Frangelico
1/2 oz. hot water

Build. Top with whipped cream.

Hot Shot

3/4 oz. Jameson Irish whiskey
3/4 oz. Baileys Irish Cream
1/2 oz. hot coffee

Build.

Hot Shot #2

3/4 oz. Grand Marnier
3/4 oz. Baileys Irish Cream
1/2 oz. coffee

Hot Shot #3

1/2 oz. Stolichnaya vodka
1/2 oz. Rumple Minze peppermint
  schnapps

Top with a few drops of Tabasco sauce.
Build.

Hot Shot #4

1 oz. Hiram Walker sambuca
1/2 oz. Carolans Irish Cream
splash coffee

Build.

Hot Stuff

1 oz. Hiram Walker amaretto
1 oz. coffee

Serve in 2 oz. shot glass.

Hot Tamale

3/4 oz. cinnamon schnapps
1/2 oz. Cuervo Gold tequila

Build.

Hot Tamale #2

Goldschlager cinnamon schnapps
grenadine

Blend with ice and serve in a shot glass.
Garnish with red-hot candies.

I Love Lucy

3/4 oz. Malibu rum
3/4 oz. sloe gin
splash orange juice
splash sprite

Pam Payton
St. Roberts, MO

Ice Blue Aqua Velva

3/4 oz. Bombay gin
3/4 oz. Stolichnaya vodka
1/2 oz. blue curacao
splash 7-Up

Shake with ice. Top with 7-Up.

Ice Caps

3/4 oz. Rumple Minze peppermint schnapps
3/4 oz. Absolut vodka

Shake with ice and strain.

Ice Pick

1 part Stolichnaya vodka
3 parts iced tea
1 splash sour mix

Build.

Iceberg Shooter

1/2 oz. Hiram Walker peppermint schnapps
1 1/2 oz. Frïs vodka

Shake with ice and strain. Serve straight up.

Icebreaker

1 oz. Rumple Minze peppermint schnapps
1 oz. Yukon Jack

Build.

Iced Blues

1 oz. blueberry schnapps
1/2 oz. blue curacao

Shake with ice and strain.

Alice Shank
Natalie's
Syracuse, NY

Ice Orgasm

1/3 Wile Spirit
1/3 Permafrost
1/3 Southern Comfort

Pour equal amounts to fill 1 oz. shot glass.
Drizzle Carolans on top. Shoot and enjoy!

Glenda Posey & Dianan Larkins
Rogers, AR

Illusion Shooter

1 part Absolut vodka
1 part peach schnapps
1 splash orange juice
1 splash cranberry juice

Shake with ice and strain.

Indian Summer

1/2 oz. Stolichnaya vodka
1/2 oz. Kahlúa
1/2 oz. pineapple juice

Shake with ice and strain.

Ink Spot

3/4 oz. blackberry brandy
1/4 oz. Rumple Minze peppermint schnapps

Shake with ice and strain.

Inkwell Surfer

2 oz. Berry Tattoo schnapps
1 oz. Malibu rum
grenadine
pineapple juice
splash 7-Up

Chill over ice.

Anita Kurek
Carney, MD

International

3/4 oz. Liquore Galliano
1/2 oz. Asbach Uralt

Shake with ice and strain.

International Incident

1/4 oz. Absolut vodka
1/4 oz. Kahlúa
1/4 oz. Disaronno amaretto
1/4 oz. Frangelico
1/4 oz. Baileys Irish Cream

Shake with ice and strain.

Irish Brogue

1 oz. Jameson Irish whiskey
1/4 oz. Irish Mist liqueur

Build.

Irish Charlie

1 oz. Baileys Irish Cream
1 oz. white crème de menthe

Stir with ice and strain into cordial glass.

Irish Flag

1 oz. green crème de menthe
1 oz. Baileys Irish Cream
1 oz. Grand Marnier

Layer in order in cordial glass.

Irish Frog

3/4 oz. Midori melon liqueur
3/4 oz. Baileys Irish Cream, chilled

Build.

Irish Frost

1 1/2 oz. Baileys Irish Cream
1 splash Coco Lopéz Crème of coconut
1 splash half & half

Shake with ice and strain.

Irish Headlock

1 oz. Baileys Irish Cream
1/4 oz. Jameson Irish whiskey
1/4 oz. Disaronno amaretto
1/4 oz. brandy

Build.

Irish Kiss

1 oz. Baileys Irish Cream
1/2 oz. Jameson Irish whiskey
1/2 oz. Irish Mist liqueur

Shake with ice and strain.

Irish Melon Ball

3/4 oz. Baileys Irish Cream
1/2 oz. Midori melon liqueur
1/2 oz. vodka

Build.

Irish Quaalude

1/2 oz. Frïs vodka
1/2 oz. Hiram Walker white crème de cacao
1/2 oz. Carolans Irish Cream
1/2 oz. Frangelico

Shake with ice and strain.

Irish Raspberry

1 part Chambord
1 part Devonshire Royal Cream liqueur

Shake with ice and strain.

Irish Rule

1 part Carolans Irish Cream
1 part Irish Mist liqueur

Build.

Irish Setter

1/2 oz. Irish Mist liqueur
1/2 oz. Frangelico
1/4 oz. Rumple Minze peppermint
  schnapps
1/4 oz. brandy

Build.

Irish Sleeper

1 oz. Jameson Irish whiskey
1/2 oz. Irish Mist liqueur
1/2 oz. Grand Marnier

Shake with ice and strain.

Iron Butterfly

1/2 oz. Kahlúa
1/2 oz. Fris vodka
1/2 oz. Carolans Irish Cream

Shake with ice and strain. Serve straight up.

Iron Cross

3/4 oz. Rumple Minze peppermint schnapps
3/4 oz. apricot brandy

Shake with ice and strain.

It Don't Matter

1 3/4 oz. Wild Turkey bourbon
float Grand Marnier

Italian Flag Shooter

1 part crème de strawberry
1 part green crème de menthe
1 part Baileys Irish Cream

Layer in order.

Italian Root Beer
(Root Beer Shooter)

Liquore Galliano
cola

Equal parts.

Italian Russian

1/2 oz. Romana sambuca
1 oz. Stolichnaya vodka

Build.

Italian Spear

1 part Hiram Walker peppermint schnapps
1 part Hiram Walker amaretto liqueur

Build.

Jack Frost

1 oz. Jack Daniel's whiskey
1 oz. peppermint schnapps

Jack O'Lantern

1/2 oz. Southern Comfort
1/2 oz. amaretto
1/2 oz. orange juice
1/2 oz. pineapple juice
grenadine

Dash of grenadine to color. Shake with ice
and strain.

Jack Rabbit

3/4 oz. Yukon Jack
1/2 oz. cherry brandy

Shake with ice and strain.

Jagasm

Absolut vodka
Kahlúa
amaretto
Jagermeister
splash Baileys Irish Cream
splash grenadine

Equal parts. Shake, top with heavy cream.

Jager Barrel

Jagermeister
root beer schnapps
cola

Build.

Jager Eraser

1 part Jagermeister
1 part Absolut vodka
soda

Build.

Jager Monster

1 part Jagermeister
2 parts orange juice
1 dash grenadine

Shake with crushed ice until smooth and strain.

Jager Vacation

1 part Jagermeister
1 part Captain Morgan coconut rum
2 parts pineapple juice

Shake with ice and strain.

Jagerita

1/2 oz. Jagermeister
1/2 oz. tequila
1/2 oz. Cointreau
juice of 1/2 lime

Shake. Strain into shot glass with salted rim.

Jager-ita

1/4 oz. Jagermeister
3/4 oz. triple sec
1/4 oz. Rose's lime juice
1/4 oz. sour mix

Kim Andersen
New York, NY

Jagertee Hot Shot

Stroh Jagertee
hot water

Equal parts. Serve in a shot glass.

Jamaican 10 Speed

1/2 oz. Midori melon liqueur
1/2 oz. Malibu rum
1/2 oz. crème de banana
1/2 oz. pineapple juice
1/2 oz. milk or cream

Keyhole Bar & Grill
Mackinaw City, MI

Jamaican Dust

3/4 oz. Puerto Rican rum
3/4 oz. Tia Maria
splash pineapple juice

Build.

Jamaican Lollipop Shooter

1 1/2 oz. crème de banana
1/2 oz. Bacardi 151 rum

Shake with ice and strain.

Jamaican Sunrise

3/4 oz. triple sec
3/4 oz. Myers's rum cream liqueur
1/2 oz. sour mix

Shake with ice and strain.

Jamaican Surfer

2 parts Malibu
1 part Tia Maria
2 parts cream

Shake with ice and strain.

Jambalaya

1/2 oz. peach schnapps
1/2 oz. Southern Comfort
1/2 oz. sweet & sour mix
drop grenadine

Gina & Janet
The Approach
Saddleback Lanes
Mission Viejo, CA

Jaw Breaker

1 1/2 oz. Goldschlager cinnamon schnapps
dash Tabasco

Shake with ice and strain.

Je Taime

3/4 oz. B&B liqueur
3/4 oz. Absolut vodka

Build.

Jeckyl & Hyde

1 oz. Jagermeister, cold
1 oz. Dr. McGillicuddy's Mentholmint, cold

Layer in test tube shot glass.

Joe Willett
Scottsdale, AZ

Jefferson Blues

1 part blue curacao
1 part wilderberry schnapps
1 part Absolut vodka
1 part Rose's sour mix
splash Sprite or 7-Up

Shake with ice and strain.

Lori Johnson
Jefferson Grille
Warwick, RI

Jell-O Shots
1 cup tequila/vodka/gin/rum, etc. (your choice)
1 box lime Jell-O brand gelatin
1 cup boiling water
3-4 oz. lime juice

In a bowl, add liquor and boiling water to gelatin. Stir until gelatin has dissolved. Chill to set. Serve in paper soufflé cups.

Jelly Bean
1 part anisette
1 part blackberry brandy
1 part Southern Comfort

Build.

Jelly Bean #2
1/3 oz. grenadine
1/3 oz. anisette
1/3 oz. tequila

Jelly Bean #3
3/4 oz. blackberry brandy
3/4 oz. amaretto
1/4 oz. Southern Comfort

Top with Southern Comfort. Build.

Jelly Bean #4

1 oz. blackberry brandy
3/4 oz. Romana sambuca

Build.

Jelly Bean #5

3/4 oz. Southern Comfort
1/2 oz. anisette
1/2 oz. grenadine

Build.

Jelly Donut

1 oz. Hiram Walker black raspberry
    schnapps
1/2 oz. half & half

Shake with ice and strain.

Jelly Fish

3/4 oz. Romana sambuca
3/4 oz. Baileys Irish Cream
3 drops grenadine

Build.

Jelly Fish #2

1 part white crème de cacao
1 part Baileys Irish Cream
1 part Disaronno amaretto
1 dash grenadine

Dash grenadine in center.

Jethro Tull Flute

1 oz. Finlandia vodka
1 oz. DeKuyper Peachtree schnapps
1/2 oz. triple sec
splash pineapple juice

Bonnie S. Bailey
Wappingers Falls, NY

Jimmy's Juice

1/2 oz. Malibu
1/2 oz. Captain Morgan spiced rum
1/2 oz. pineapple juice
1/2 oz. cranberry juice

Shake with ice and strain.

Johnny on the Beach

1 1/2 oz. Finlandia vodka
1 oz. Midori melon liqueur
1 oz. Chambord
1/2 oz. pineapple juice
1/2 oz. orange juice
1/2 oz. grapefruit juice
1/2 oz. cranberry juice

Shake with ice and strain. Serves two.

Jolly Rancher

1 oz. peach schnapps
1/2 oz. apple schnapps
1/2 oz. cranberry juice

Shake with ice and strain.

Jolly Rancher #2

1/2 oz. Midori melon liqueur
1/2 oz. peach schnapps
1 oz. cranberry juice

Shake with ice and strain.

Juicy Fruit

1 oz. vodka
1/4 oz. peach schnapps
1/4 oz. Midori melon liqueur
1/2 oz. pineapple juice

Shake with ice and strain.

Junior Mint

3/4 oz. Godiva
3/4 oz. Rumple Minze

John Kyle
Pittsburgh, PA

K.O. Pectate

1/3 oz. Kahlúa
1/3 oz. peppermint schnapps
1/3 oz. cream

Kahlúa Surfer

1 part Kahlúa
2 parts Malibu
1 part cream

Shake with ice and strain.

Kaisermeister

root beer schnapps
Jagermeister

Equal parts. Shake with ice and strain.

Kamikazi

1 1/2 oz. Stolichnaya vodka
1/4 oz. Cointreau
splash Rose's lime juice

Shake with ice and strain.

Kandy Kane

1 part Rumple Minze peppermint schnapps
1 part Hiram Walker crème de noyaux

Build.

Kaytusha Rocker

1 oz. Frïs vodka
1/2 oz. Kahlúa
1 dash cream
1 oz. pineapple juice

Shake with ice and strain.

Keno Koolaid

1/2 oz. Southern Comfort
1/2 oz. vodka
1/4 oz. triple sec
1/4 oz. Chambord
1/4 oz. grenadine

Lisa Nadolny & Ken Santos
Narragansett, RI

Kentucky Colonel

1 oz. Wild Turkey 101 bourbon
1/4 oz. Benedictine

Shake with ice and strain.

Key Largo Punch

3/4 oz. Key Largo Tropical schnapps
3/4 oz. Malibu
Equal parts:
   cranberry juice
   pineapple juice
splash grenadine

Shake with ice and strain.

Scott Karg
Loughlins Chesapeake Pub
Edgewood, MD

Key Lime High

1/2 oz. Liquore Galliano
1/2 oz. Cointreau
1/2 oz. orange juice
splash lime
splash half & half

Shake with ice and strain. Makes two.

Key Lime Pie

1 1/2 oz. Licor 43
dash Rose's lime juice
dash sweet and sour mix
1/2 oz. cream

Shake with ice and strain.

Kicken Chicken

3/4 oz. Wild Turkey 101 bourbon
3/4 oz. Rumple Minze peppermint schnapps

Shake with ice and strain.

Killer Bee

3/4 oz. Jagermeister
3/4 oz. Barenjager apple schnapps

Shake with ice and strain.

Killer Kool Aid

1 oz. Absolut vodka
1/4 oz. Disaronno amaretto
1/4 oz. Midori melon liqueur
1/2 oz. cranberry juice

Shake with ice and strain.

Killer Oreos

Jagermeister
Kahlúa
Baileys Irish Cream

Equal parts. Shake with ice and strain.

Kilt Lifter

1 part Baileys Irish Cream
1 part butterscotch schnapps

Build.

King Alphonse

1 1/2 oz. dark crème de cacao
1/2 oz. cream

Build.

Kiss in the Dark

3/4 oz. Tanqueray gin
3/4 oz. cherry brandy
1/4 oz. dry vermouth

Shake with ice and strain.

Kiwi Kicker

1/2 oz. Midori melon liqueur
1/2 oz. Yukon Jack
1/2 oz. Disaronno amaretto
cranberry juice
pineapple juice

Shake with ice and strain. Fill with juice.

Scott Karg
Loughlins Chesapeake Pub
Edgewood, MD

Knickerbocker

1/2 oz. Kahlúa
1/2 oz. Hiram Walker amaretto
1/2 oz. Frïs vodka
1/2 oz. Hiram Walker peppermint schnapps

Shake with ice and strain.

Kool Aid

3/4 oz. Midori melon liqueur
3/4 oz. amaretto
1/2 oz. cranberry juice

Shake with ice and strain.

Krazy Kool-Aid

1 part Finlandia cranberry vodka
1 part Disaronno amaretto
1 part Midori melon liqueur

Shake with ice and strain.

Kurant Affair

1 oz. Absolut Kurant vodka
1/2 oz. pineapple juice
splash cranberry juice

Use just a touch of cranberry juice.

Kurant Kooler

1 1/4 oz. Absolut Kurant vodka
1/2 oz. sweet & sour mix
splash 7-Up

Shake Kurant and sweet & sour mix. Top with 7-Up.

Kurant Shooter

1/2 oz. Absolut Kurant vodka
1/2 oz. Midori melon liqueur
1 oz. pineapple juice

Shake with ice and strain.

La Cucaracha

1/2 oz. Kahlúa
1/2 oz. Cuervo tequila
1/2 oz. bottled mineral water

Build.

Lady Godiva

3/4 oz. Grand Marnier
3/4 oz. Kahlúa
1/2 oz. cream

Shake with ice and strain.

Lala's Lumps

1 part Finlandia vodka
1 part Root Beer schnapps

Build.

Landshark

1 1/4 oz. Stubbs Australian rum
3/4 oz. Malibu
pineapple juice
splash grenadine

Shake with ice and strain.

Landslide

1/3 crème de banana
1/3 Disaronno amaretto
1/3 Baileys Irish Cream

Shake with ice and strain.

Laser Beam

1/2 oz. Jack Daniel's black whiskey
1/2 oz. Rumple Minze peppermint
   schnapps
1/4 oz. Drambuie

Shake with ice and strain.

Laser Beam #2

3/4 oz. Jack Daniel's whiskey
1/2 oz. anisette
dash grenadine

Shake with ice and strain.

Lava Lamp

2/3 Rumple Minze peppermint schnapps
1/3 Absolut Peppar vodka
7 drops Tabasco sauce

Use very cold Rumple Minze. Drop in
Tabasco carefully to form floating balls in
the middle of liqueur. Serve with cold draft
beer back.

Jessica Lee
International Cocktail Lounge
San Francisco, CA

Leg Spreader Shooter

1 part Kahlúa
1 part Liquore Galliano

Shake with ice and strain.

Lemon Drop

1 1/4 oz. Absolut Citron vodka

Serve with a wedge of lemon coated with sugar. Shoot the Absolut Citron, then suck the lemon.

Lemon Drop #2

1 oz. Absolut Citron vodka
1/2 oz. orange juice

Shake with ice and strain.

Lemon Drop #3

1 oz. Stolichnaya vodka
dash Cointreau

Place lemon wheel over shot glass. Top with powdered sugar.

Lemonade Cactus

1 oz. DeKuyper cactus juice
1 oz. lemonade

Shake with ice and strain.

Leprechaun Shooter

3/4 oz. blue curacao
3/4 oz. peach schnapps
3/4 oz. orange juice

Shake with ice and strain.

Lethal Weapon

1 oz. Finlandia vodka
1/2 oz. peach schnapps
1 splash cranberry juice
1 splash Rose's lime juice

Shake with ice and strain.

Licorice Stick

3/4 oz. Licor 43
1/2 oz. Cointreau
1/2 oz. cream
dash sour mix

Shake with ice and strain.

Licorice Stick #2

1 1/4 oz. Stolichnaya vodka
1/2 oz. Hiram Walker anisette
1/4 oz. triple sec

Shake with ice and strain.

Licorice Lix

3/4 oz. sambuca
1/4 oz. orange juice

Life Saver

1 part Malibu
1 part Smirnoff vodka
1 part Midori melon liqueur
1 part 7-Up or Sprite (optional)

Build.

Lighthouse

1 part Kahlúa
1 part Bacardi 151 rum

Build.

Lion Tamer

3/4 oz. Southern Comfort
1/4 oz. Rose's lime juice

Fill mixing glass with ice. Add Southern Comfort and lime juice. Stir. Strain into a chilled shot glass.

Liquid Babysitter

1/2 oz. Absolut vodka
1/2 oz. Captain Morgan
splash cherry pucker
splash grape pucker
splash apple pucker
splash watermelon pucker
splash 7-Up

Christin "CK" Kotila
Warren, MI

Liquid Cocaine

1/2 oz. Southern Comfort
1/2 oz. Disaronno amaretto
1/2 oz. Grand Marnier
splash orange juice
splash pineapple juice

Shake with ice and strain.

Liquid Nitrogen

Romana sambuca
No. 12 ouzo

Mix equal parts and strain over ice.

Liquid Quaalude

1 1/2 oz. Stolichnaya vodka
1/4 oz. Southern Comfort
1/8 oz. crème de noyaux
1/2 splash orange juice
1/2 splash pineapple juice

Shake with ice and strain.

Liquid Valium

1 1/4 oz. Fris vodka
1/2 oz. Hiram Walker peppermint schnapps

Shake with ice and strain. Serve in 2 oz. shooter.

Little Beer

3/4 oz. Licor 43
1/4 oz. half & half

Float half & half on top.

Little Purple Man

1 oz. sambuca
1 oz. Chambord raspberry liqueur

197

Loch Ness Monster

3/4 oz. Midori melon liqueur
3/4 oz. Baileys Irish Cream
1/4 oz. Jagermeister

Build.

Loco Lobo

Liquore Galliano
Cuervo tequila
lime juice

Equal parts.

Locomotive Breath

1/2 oz. Bacardi dark rum
1 oz. J&B Scotch
1 oz. Jose Cuervo tequila
splash ginger ale

Stir, don't shake. Pour into highball (no ice).

Bonnie S. Bailey
Wappingers Falls, NY

Long Island Shooter

1 part Absolut vodka
1 part Beefeater gin
1 part Cuervo tequila
1 part Bacardi rum
1 part triple sec
1 part sour mix
1 splash Coke

Shake with ice and strain, top with Coke.

Loose Moose

1/2 oz. Liquore Galliano
1/2 oz. peach schnapps
1/4 oz. triple sec

Splash of lemonade and chill in 2 oz. shot glass.

Lounge Lizard

2 parts Myers's Original dark rum
1 part pineapple juice
1 part orange juice
1 part sour mix
1 splash grenadine

Shake with ice and strain.

Love Bite

1 1/4 oz. Koko Kanu coconut rum schnapps

Poured over a chocolate candy kiss in a shot glass.

Peter Martin Associates, Inc.
Stamford, CT

Love Potion #9

3/4 oz. cherry brandy
3/4 oz. Rumple Minze peppermint schnapps
1 oz. cranberry juice

Shake with ice and strain.

Love Shack

1 1/4 oz. Myers's Original dark rum
1/4 oz. orange juice
1/4 oz. grenadine
7-Up

Build. Top with 7-Up.

Lucky Seven

Equal parts:
   vodka
   amaretto
   Bacardi 151
   Jack Daniel's
   Southern Comfort
   sloe gin
splash cranberry juice
splash lime juice
splash orange juice

Serve in a very big shot glass.

Joel Gagne
Lowell, MA

Lust in the Dust

1/4 oz. Kahlúa
3/4 oz. Original Bartenders Hot Sex

Susie Viles
Denison, TX

Lymbo

1/2 oz. Bacardi dark rum
1/2 oz. Hiram Walker cinnamon schnapps
1/2 oz. tequila
splash Tabasco

Shake with ice and strain.

Noreen Maes
Luckie's
Sparks, NV

Lynchburg Lemonade Shooter

3/4 oz. Jack Daniel's
1/4 oz. triple sec
1/2 oz. sour mix

Shake with ice and strain.

M&M

1 oz. Kahlúa
1 oz. Disaronno amaretto

Build.

M.D. Pepper

1 part amaretto
1 part Bacardi 151 rum
1 part beer

Build.

Mad Cow

3/4 oz. Opal Nera sambuca
1/4 oz. Godiva chocolate liqueur
splash milk

David "Buckwheat" Cavaliere
N. Providence, RI

Madras Shooter

1 oz. Absolut vodka
1/2 oz. orange juice
1/2 oz. cranberry juice

Substitute grapefruit juice for orange juice
and it's a Sea Breeze Shooter. Build.

Malibu Classic

1 oz. Stolichnaya vodka
1/2 oz. Malibu
1/4 oz. cranberry juice
1/4 oz. orange juice

Shake with ice and strain.

Malibu Sex on the Beach

1/2 oz. Hiram Walker peach schnapps
1/2 oz. Frïs vodka
1/2 oz. cranberry juice

Stir with ice and strain.

Marie Brizard Ecstasy

1 part Marie Brizard cherry liqueur
1 part Marie Brizard peach liqueur
1 part Marie Brizard pear liqueur

Fill to top with orange juice; add a splash of
cranberry juice. Build.

Marie Brizard Sun 'N Fun

1 part Marie Brizard triple sec
1 part Marie Brizard coconut liqueur
1 part Marie Brizard mango liqueur

Build. Fill the balance of the shooter tube or glass with pineapple juice. Pour a drop of grenadine on top. Shoot!

Masconivich Shooter

1/3 Courvoisier cognac
1/3 Hiram Walker triple sec
1/3 brandy

On rindless lemon wheel—one side sugar, one side instant coffee. Bite wheel and shoot drink! Serve in pony or cordial glass.

Matador

1 oz. Licor 43
1 oz. Jagermeister, cold

Serve in a shifter glass.

Alfonso Buceta
Stroudsburg, PA

Mattapoo

1 oz. Smirnoff vodka
1/2 oz. Midori melon liqueur
1/4 oz. pineapple juice
1/4 oz. grapefruit juice

Shake with ice and strain.

Maureen's Jellybean

dash of ouzo
1 1/2 parts Echte Kroatzbeere blackberry
   liqueur

Float ouzo on top.

Me and My Gal

Liquore Galliano
Midori melon liqueur
cranberry juice

Equal parts.

Meat & Potatoes

1 1/2 parts Rimanto Potato vodka

Fill shot glass with cold Rimanto; garnish
with generous slice of pepperoni.

Melon Ball

2 parts Midori melon liqueur
1 part Finlandia vodka
3 parts pineapple juice

Shake with ice and strain.

Melon Ball #2

3/4 oz. Midori melon liqueur
1/2 oz. Absolut vodka
1/4 oz. pineapple juice
1/4 oz. orange juice

Shake with ice and strain.

Melon Snowball

3/4 oz. Frïs vodka
3/4 oz. Midori melon liqueur
1/2 oz. pineapple juice
dash cream

Serve with crushed ice in shot glass.

Melonnium or Shannon's Sweet (Sur)prize

1/2 oz. Malibu rum
1/2 oz. Midori
1/2 oz. watermelon pucker
pineapple juice
splash 7-Up

Shannon Frenzen
Genoa, NE

Memphis Belle

1 oz. Baileys Irish Cream
1 oz. Southern Comfort

Build.

Mexican Berry

1 part Chambord
1 part Cuervo tequila

Build.

Mexican Chiller

3/4 oz. tequila
1/4 oz. clamato juice
drop Tabasco

Mexican Flag

1/2 oz. grenadine
1/2 oz. green crème de menthe
1/2 oz. Baileys Irish Cream

Build.

Mexican Flag #2

1/2 oz. sloe gin
1/2 oz. vodka
1/2 oz. Midori melon liqueur

Pour sloe gin into a shot glass. Float vodka on top, then Midori on top of that.

Mexican Grandberry

1 oz. Cuervo tequila
1/4 oz. Grand Marnier
1/4 oz. Chambord
1/2 oz. sour mix

Shake with ice and strain.

Mexican Missile

3/4 oz. Cuervo tequila
3/4 oz. Green Chartreuse liqueur
dash Tabasco

Combine tequila and Chartreuse in a shot glass. Add dash of Tabasco to season.

Midnight Sun

1 1/4 oz. Finlandia cranberry vodka
1/2 oz. Kahlúa

Shake with ice and strain.

Midori Kamikaze

3 parts Midori melon liqueur
1 splash triple sec
1 part Rose's lime juice

Shake with ice and serve.

Mikey Mike

1 oz. Malibu
1/2 oz. DeKuyper Peachtree schnapps
1/2 oz. Chambord
Equal parts:
  orange juice
  pineapple juice

Michael Manosh
Providence, RI

Miles of Smiles

1/3 Seagram's V.O.
1/3 Disaronno amaretto
1/3 Rumple Minze peppermint schnapps

Build.

Milk of Amnesia

1/2 Baileys Irish Cream
1/2 Jagermeister

Build.

Milky Way

1/2 oz. amaretto
1/2 oz. dark crème de cacao
1 oz. whipped cream

Shake with ice and strain.

Milky Way #2

1/2 oz. Smirnoff vodka
1/2 oz. Kahlúa
1/4 oz. dark crème de cacao
3/4 oz. whipped cream

Shake with ice and strain.

Milky Way #3

3/4 oz. Kahlúa
1/2 oz. Baileys Irish Cream
1/2 oz. Tuaca
dash cream

Todd Osterhouse
Austin, TX

Milwaukee River

1/2 oz. Kahlúa
1/2 oz. blue curacao
1/2 oz. Baileys Irish Cream

Build.

Mind Collapse

1/2 oz. Jameson Irish whiskey
1/2 oz. Hiram Walker peppermint schnapps
1/2 oz. Jagermeister

Shake with ice and strain.

Mind Eraser

1 part Stolichnaya vodka
1 part Kahlúa
1 part soda water

Build.

Mini Margarita

1 part Sauza tequila
1 part Cointreau

Serve in a test tube and garnish with a lime
wedge.

Mini Martini

1/3 oz. French vermouth
1/3 oz. Italian vermouth
1/3 oz. gin
4 dashes Absente

John F. Pflugh
Rollioux, CA

Mint Julep

1 oz. Maker's Mark bourbon
1/2 oz. Hiram Walker green crème de
 menthe

Build.

Mint-2-Lips

1/4 oz. green crème de menthe
1/2 oz. crème de cacao
1/4 oz. rum
1/2 oz. Baileys Irish Cream
1/4 oz. milk

Teri Blinson
Tempe, AZ

Misdemeanor

1/2 oz. DeKuyper Butterschnapps
1/2 oz. Crown Royal

Big Kel
Peoria, IL

Missing Link

1 part Romana black sambuca
1 part Rumple Minze peppermint schnapps
1 part Jagermeister

Build.

Kam S. Yu
Chopsticks Restaurant
Leominster, MA

Mission Accomplished

2 oz. Smirnoff vodka
1/2 oz. Cointreau
1/4 oz. Rose's lime juice
dash grenadine

Shake with ice and strain. Serves two.

Misty Dew

1 oz. Irish Mist liqueur
1 oz. Tullamore Dew Irish whiskey

Mona's Man

1/2 oz. Mt. Gay rum
1/2 oz. Disaronno amaretto
1/2 oz. Malibu
1/4 oz. orange juice
1/4 oz. pineapple juice

Shake with ice and strain.

Monkey Gland

1 oz. Bombay gin
1/4 oz. Benedictine brandy
dash grenadine
dash orange juice

Shake with ice and strain.

Monkey Poop

3/4 oz. vodka
3/4 oz. crème de banana
splash orange juice
splash pineapple juice
dash Rose's lime juice

Shake with ice and strain.

Monkey See–Monkey Do

1 part Myers's Original dark rum
1 part banana liqueur
1 part Baileys Irish Cream
3 parts orange juice

Shake with ice and strain.

Monkey Wrench

1 oz. Bacardi rum
1/2 oz. orange juice
1/2 oz. sour mix
dash grenadine

Shake with ice and strain. Float dash grenadine.

Monkey's Lunch

3/4 oz. Kahlúa
1/2 oz. crème de banana
1/2 oz. Myers's rum cream liqueur

Build.

Monk's Slide

Frangelico
Tuaca
Baileys Irish Cream

Equal parts. Build.

Jennifer Mills
Pescatore Italian Restaurant
Hilo, HI

Monsoon

1/4 oz. Kahlúa
1/4 oz. Hiram Walker amaretto
1/4 oz. Frïs vodka
1/4 oz. Carolans Irish Cream
1/4 oz. Frangelico

Build.

Moody Blue

1/3 oz. amaretto
1/3 oz. blueberry schnapps
1/3 oz. gin

Morgan's Jolly Roger

1 part Captain Morgan spiced rum
1 part cinnamon schnapps

Build.

Morgan's Wench

1 part Captain Morgan spiced rum
1 part Disaronno amaretto
float dark crème de cacao

Build.

Mother Load

1/3 Absolut vodka
1/3 Leroux blackberry brandy
1/3 Malibu

Build.

Vannie Ness
Gordy's Tavern
Kenosha, WI

Mother's Milk

light rum
amaretto
Kahlúa
Southern Comfort
Baileys Irish Cream
Grand Marnier

Equal parts. Shake with ice and strain.

Alvah L. Knapp
The West End Hotel Inc.
Hamburg, NY

Mounds Bar

1 part Malibu
1 part dark crème de cacao
1 part Baileys Irish Cream
1 part cream (optional)

For extra chocolate flavor, try adding Mozart chocolate liqueur.

Mr. Wilson

3/4 oz. apple schnapps
3/4 oz. Malibu
3/4 oz. cranberry juice
3/4 oz. orange juice

Shake with ice and strain.

Mud Slide

1 part Frïs vodka
1 part Kahlúa
1 part Carolans Irish Cream

Build. Add Hiram Walker hazelnut liqueur and it's called a Mississippi Mud Pie.

Mustang Sally

1 oz. Absolut vodka
1 oz. Malibu rum
Equal parts:
  orange juice
  cranberry juice

Holly Basky
Denver, CO

Mystery Madness

1 oz. Bacardi rum
1/2 oz. blue curacao
splash sour mix

Kimberly Picazio
Uncasville, CT

Naked Barbie Doll

1 oz. Malibu rum
1/2 oz. Bols strawberry liqueur
pineapple juice

Marty Waatt
Atlantic City, NJ

Naked Politician

Bacardi
Captain Morgan
Myers's
Malibu rum
splash banana liqueur
splash orange juice & pineapple juice
dash grenadine

Michael Morin
Boston, MA

Napalm Bomb

3/4 oz. Chambord
3/4 oz. Smirnoff vodka
1/2 oz. pineapple juice

Shake with ice and strain.

Nashville Shooter

1 1/2 oz. Absolut vodka
1 splash sour mix
1 splash cranberry juice
1/2 splash Rose's lime juice

Shake with ice and strain.

Nasty Lori

1 part Cuervo tequila
1 part peach schnapps
1 part pineapple juice

Shake with ice and strain.

Lori A. Martin
Fort Dick, CA

Negroni Shooter

1 part Bombay gin
1 part Campari
1 part sweet vermouth
1 splash seltzer/club soda

Build.

Neon Cactus

1 oz. DeKuyper cactus juice
2 oz. Rose's lime juice

Shake with ice and strain.

Nepa Shooter

1/2 oz. Stoli Ohranj vodka
1/2 oz. Absolut Kurant
1/2 oz. Malibu rum
1/4 oz. Cointreau
1/2 oz. pineapple juice
splash Chambord

Robert Rothlein
St. Petersburg, FL

Nero's Delight

Romana sambuca
Baileys Irish Cream

Equal parts layered in shot glass.

224

Nettie's Knockout

1 1/2 oz. Midori melon liqueur
1/2 oz. triple sec
splash Squirt

Frontier City Saloon
Charlotte, MI

Neutron Blaster

1/2 oz. Kahlúa
1/2 oz. Grand Marnier
1/2 oz. Disaronno amaretto
1/2 oz. Baileys Irish Cream

Shake with ice and strain.

New York Slammer

1/2 oz. amaretto
1/4 oz. sloe gin
1/2 oz. Southern Comfort
1/4 oz. Cointreau
1/2 oz. orange juice

Shake with ice and strain.

Night Moves

1/4 oz. Kahlúa
1/4 oz. Baileys Irish Cream
1/4 oz. vanilla schnapps
1/4 oz. buttershots schnapps
1/4 oz. Captain Morgan spiced rum

Pam Hunter
Frankfort, IN

Nighthawk

1 oz. Myers's Original dark rum
1 oz. Rumple Minze peppermint schnapps

Build.

Nightmare Shooter

3/4 oz. Bombay gin
3/4 oz. Dubonnet
1/4 oz. cherry brandy
1 splash orange juice

Shake with ice and strain.

Ninety Nine (99)

1 oz. Carolans Irish Cream
1 oz. Tullamore Dew

Stir with ice and serve straight up.

Ninja

3/4 oz. Kahlúa
1/2 oz. Midori melon liqueur
3/4 oz. Frangelico

Build.

Ninja Turtle

1 part Crystal Comfort liqueur
1 part Midori melon liqueur
1 part sour mix
2 parts pineapple juice

Shake with ice and strain. If you don't have
Crystal Comfort, use Southern Comfort.

Northern Exposure

Malibu rum
Canadian Mist

Equal parts. Build.

Saraj Amann
Evansville, WI

Not

1/4 part Opal Nera black sambuca
1/4 part ouzo
1/4 part tequila

Build.

Vannie Ness
Gordy's Bar
Kenosha, WI

Nuclear Accelerator

1/2 oz. Frïs vodka
1/2 oz. Hiram Walker peppermint schnapps
1/2 oz. Grand Marnier

Build.

Nuclear Holocaust

1 part Mt. Gay rum
1 part peach schnapps
1 part blue curacao
1 part banana schnapps
1 part cranberry juice

Shake with ice and strain.

PJ Joelting
Kansas City, MO

Numero Uno

1 oz. Sauza Conmemorativo tequila
1/2 oz. Hiram Walker triple sec

Shake with ice and strain.

Nut Cracker

1 part Frangelico
1 part Rumple Minze peppermint schnapps
1 part Myers's rum cream liqueur

Shake with ice and strain.

Nut Cracker #2

3/4 oz. Stolichnaya vodka
3/4 oz. Frangelico
1/2 oz. cream

Build.

Nut Slammer

1/4 oz. Absolut
1/4 oz. Kahlúa
1/4 oz. amaretto
1/4 oz. Frangelico
1/2 oz. milk or half & half

Nuts & Berries

1/2 oz. Chambord
1/2 oz. Baileys Irish Cream
1/2 oz. Frangelico
1/2 oz. cream

Shake with ice and strain.

Nutty Irishman

1/2 oz. Frangelico
1/2 oz. Baileys Irish Cream

Build.

Nutty Jamaican

3/4 oz. Frangelico
1 oz. Myers's rum cream liqueur

Shake with ice and strain.

Nutty Professor

1/2 oz. Grand Marnier
1/2 oz. Frangelico
1/2 oz. Baileys Irish Cream

Stir and strain.

Nutty Surfer

1 part Frangelico
2 parts Malibu
1 part cream

Shake with ice and strain.

Oatmeal Cookie

1 oz. Baileys Irish Cream
1 oz. Frangelico
1/4 oz. Goldschlager cinnamon schnapps

Shake with ice and strain.

Oatmeal Cookie #2

1/4 Jagermeister
1/4 Kahlúa
1/4 Baileys Irish Cream
1/4 butterscotch schnapps

Shake with ice and strain.

O'Casey Scotch Terrier

1 part Baileys Irish Cream
1 part J&B scotch

Build.

Ocean Breeze

3/4 oz. Chambord
3/4 oz. Cointreau
1/2 oz. cranberry juice

Shake with ice and strain.

Oh My Gosh

1 oz. Disaronno amaretto
1 oz. DeKuyper Peachtree schnapps

Stir with ice and strain.

Oil Slick

3/4 oz. Rumple Minze peppermint schnapps
3/4 oz. Jagermeister

Build.

Oil Slick #2

3/4 oz. Rumple Minze peppermint schnapps
3/4 oz. Jim Beam bourbon

Build.

Oil Slick #3

3/4 parts Der Lach Original Goldwasser
splash black sambuca

Served in chilled shot glass.

Old Glory

1/3 oz. Dr. McGillicuddy's Mentholmint
    schnapps
1/3 oz. grenadine
1/3 oz. blue curacao

Build.

Old Lay

3/4 oz. Cointreau
1 1/4 oz. Jose Cuervo Gold tequila
1 dash grenadine
3/4 oz. Rose's lime juice

Shake with ice and strain.

Orange Bush

1/2 oz. Grand Marnier
1/4 oz. Smirnoff vodka
1 oz. orange juice

Shake with ice and strain.

Orange Crush

1 oz. Absolut vodka
1/2 oz. Cointreau
1/2 oz. orange juice
dash 7-Up

Shake with ice and strain. Top with 7-Up.

Orange Julius

1 oz. Disaronno amaretto
3 oz. beer
2 oz. orange juice

Serve in frosted shot glass. Serves two.

Missi Langston
San Antonio, TX

Oreo Cookie

1 part Romana black sambuca
1 part Kahlúa
1 part cream

Shake with ice and strain.

Orgasm

1 part Disaronno amaretto
1 part Kahlúa
1 part Baileys Irish Cream

Shake with ice and strain.

Orgasm #2

1 1/2 oz. Southern Comfort
1/2 oz. amaretto
3/4 oz. pineapple juice or orange juice

Shake with ice and strain.

Orgasm #3

1/4 oz. Cointreau
3/4 oz. Kahlúa
1/4 oz. Bombay gin
1/4 oz. Stolichnaya vodka
1/4 oz. Southern Comfort

Shake with ice and strain.

Orgasm #4

3/4 oz. peppermint schnapps
1/2 oz. Myers's rum cream liqueur

Build.

Orgasm #5

3/4 oz. Baileys Irish Cream
3/4 oz. Disaronno amaretto

Shake with ice and strain.

Oyster from Hell

1 oyster
Jose Cuervo tequila
3 dashes Tabasco

In a shot glass place: one raw oyster, fill with tequila, and three dashes of Tabasco.

Michael Burrell
Elegant Buns Restaurant and Bar
San Jose, CA

Oyster Shooter

3/4 shot Absolut vodka
2 splashes bloody Mary mix

Over two raw oysters pour Absolut and bloody Mary mix. Bite lemon wedge. Serve in pony or cordial glass.

Oyster Shooter #2 (A.K.A. Slimer)

1 shot Absolut Peppar vodka
1 raw oyster
1 spoonful horseradish
1 dash cocktail sauce

Mix in a shooter glass and slide it down!

Panama Jack

1 1/4 oz. Yukon Jack
3/4 oz. pineapple juice
splash club soda

Shake with ice and strain. Top with splash
of soda.

Panama Red

1 oz. Jose Cuervo Gold tequila
1/4 oz. Cointreau
1/4 oz. grenadine
1/4 oz. sour mix

Shake with ice and strain.

Pancho Villa

1/2 oz. crème de almond
1/2 oz. Cuervo white tequila
1/2 oz. Bacardi 151 rum

Layer crème de almond and tequila in shot
glass. Top with float of Bacardi 151.

Panther

3/4 oz. peach brandy
3/4 oz. white crème de menthe

Shake with ice and strain.

Panty Burner

1/3 Disaronno amaretto
1/3 Kahlúa
1/3 Frangelico

Stir with ice and strain.

Paradise

1 1/2 oz. Puerto Rican rum
1/2 oz. Hiram Walker apricot brandy

Build.

Jamie Wilson
Langley, WA

Paramedic

1 shot Absolut vodka
4 drops Tabasco sauce

Build.

Lisa Switzer
Knox American Legion
Know, PA

Paranoia

1 oz. Hiram Walker amaretto
1/2 oz. orange juice

Shake with ice and strain.

Parisian Blonde

3/4 oz. Bacardi light rum
3/4 oz. Cointreau
3/4 oz. Myers's Original dark rum

Shake with ice and strain.

Passion Cream

1 oz. white crème de cacao
1 oz. cream

Shake with ice and strain.

Patriot

1/2 oz. Liquore Galliano
1/2 oz. Kahlúa
1/2 oz. Baileys Irish Cream

Carefully float one ingredient over the other in the order above to form layers. Do not stir.

Peace in Ireland

1/2 oz. Irish Mist liqueur or Tullamore Dew
1/2 oz. Carolans Irish Cream

Shake with ice and strain.

Peach Almond Shake

1 oz. amaretto
1/2 oz. peach schnapps
1/2 oz. cream

Shake with ice and strain.

Peach Bunny

3/4 oz. DeKuyper Peachtree schnapps
3/4 oz. white crème de cacao
3/4 oz. light cream

Shake with ice and strain into cordial glass.

Peach Pirate

3/4 oz. Hiram Walker peach schnapps
1/2 oz. Bacardi rum

Build.

Peach Pit

1 part apple schnapps
1 part peach schnapps

Stir with ice and strain.

Peach Preparation

1 oz. peach schnapps
1 oz. Bacardi 151 rum

Shake with ice and strain.

Peach Tart

1 oz. DeKuyper Peachtree schnapps
1/2 oz. lime juice

Stir with ice and strain.

Peaches and Cream

3/4 oz. peach schnapps
dash Bacardi 151 rum
1/2 oz. cream

Shake with ice and strain.

Peanut Butter & Jelly

3/4 oz. Frangelico
3/4 oz. Chambord

Shake with ice and strain.

Pear Harbor

1 oz. Suntory vodka
1/4 oz. Midori melon liqueur
3/4 oz. pineapple juice

Shake with ice and strain.

Pecker Head

2/3 shot Yukon Jack
2/3 shot Disaronno amaretto
1 splash pineapple juice

Shake with ice and strain.

Pee Wee's Beamer

3/4 oz. Malibu
3/4 oz. Tangueray Stirling vodka
orange juice

Shake with ice and strain.

Penalty Shot

1 oz. Kahlúa
1 oz. Hiram Walker peppermint schnapps

Chill over ice and strain.

Tom Rock
Bartenders in the Burbs
Dedham, MA

Penetrator

1 part Liquore Galliano
1 part Absolut vodka
chilled lemon
sugar

Pour ingredients into a shooter glass. Cut
lemon and coat with sugar. Eat the lemon.

Pepper Pot

1 1/4 oz. Hiram Walker Red Hot schnapps
dash Tabasco

Shake with ice and strain. Serve straight up.

Peppermint Banana

3/4 oz. crème de banana
1/2 oz. Rumple Minze peppermint schnapps
1/4 oz. Baileys Irish Cream

In a shooter glass, combine crème de
banana and peppermint schnapps. Carefully
float Baileys on top.

Gary Elass
N. Canton, OH

Peppermint Patty

1 part Rumple Minze peppermint schnapps
1 part Kahlúa
1 part dark crème de cacao
1 splash cream

Shake with ice and strain.

Peppermint Twist

3/4 oz. Stolichnaya vodka
1/2 oz. Baileys Irish Cream
1/2 oz. Rumple Minze peppermint schnapps

Build.

Pickle Tickle

1 oz. Cuervo Gold tequila
1 oz. pickle juice

Shoot the Cuervo and chase with pickle juice.

Pile Driver

1/2 oz. J&B scotch
1/2 oz. tequila
1/2 oz. Bacardi 151 rum
dash Rose's lime juice
dash grenadine

Chill over ice and strain into shot glass. Float grenadine on top.

Michael Kirsch
Generous George's
Alexandria, VA

Pineapple Bomb

1 part Southern Comfort
1 part Disaronno amaretto
1 part pineapple juice

Add a splash of club soda if you'd like, and
suck it up quickly with a straw.

Pineapple Bomb #2

1 oz. Malibu
1/4 oz. Bacardi black rum
3/4 oz. pineapple juice

Shake with ice and strain.

Pineapple Bomb #3

3/4 oz. Captain Morgan spiced rum
3/4 oz. Southern Comfort
1/2 oz. Disaronno amaretto
1 oz. pineapple juice

Shake with ice and strain. Serves two.

Pineapple Upside Down Cake

1 oz. Finlandia vodka
1/2 oz. pineapple juice
shot whipped cream

Serve in shot glass. Top with whipped cream.

Pink Caddy

3/4 oz. Sauza tequila
3/4 oz. Licor 43
1/2 oz. cranberry juice

Shake with ice and strain.

Pink Cadillac

2 parts DeKuyper Key Largo Tropical
   schnapps
1 part Mt. Gay rum
2 parts pineapple juice
1 part cranberry juice

Shake with ice and strain.

Pink Cod

1 oz. Cuervo 1800 tequila
1/4 oz. Grand Marnier
3/4 oz. sour mix
splash cranberry juice

Shake with ice and strain.

Pink Lemonade

1 1/2 oz. Absolut Citron vodka
1/2 oz. cranberry juice
1/2 oz. sour mix

Shake with ice and strain.

Pink Nipple

1 shot Chambord
1 shot Baileys Irish Cream
1 dash grenadine

Dash grenadine to create nipple. Build.

Pink Nipple #2

1 1/2 oz. Finlandia cranberry vodka
1/4 oz. Romana sambuca

Shake with ice and strain.

Pink Petal

1 part Goldschlager
1 part Hot Damn cinnamon schnapps

Pam Bennett
Fishers Landing, NY

Pink Squirrel

1/2 oz. crème de noyaux
1/2 oz. white crème de cacao
1 oz. cream

Shake with ice and strain.

Pirates' Gold

2 parts rum
1 part Goldschlager cinnamon schnapps

Shake with ice and strain.

Korin Price
El Rancho Saloon
Steamboat Springs, CO

Pixie Stick

1 part Stoli Ohranj vodka
1 part DeKuyper grape pucker
1 part sour mix

Karl Dover
Birminghan, AL

Pleading Insanity

1/2 oz. Stolichnaya vodka
1/2 oz. Myers's Original dark rum
1/2 oz. Sauza Gold tequila

Shake with ice and strain.

Polar Bear

1/2 oz. Stolichnaya vodka
1/2 oz. white crème de cacao
1 oz. cream

Shake with ice and strain.

Polish Red Hair (Cherry Coke)

2 oz. Luksusowa vodka
1 oz. amaretto
1 oz. Rose's lime juice
2 drops grenadine
Coke

Serve in glass shaker. Put two or three
straws and drink it down with several
friends.

Missi Langston
San Antonio, TX

Ponce Appeal

shot Captain Morgan
shot Bacardi Limón
splash lemonade

Shake with ice. Strain into shot glass. Rim
with fresh lemon or squeeze of lemon.

Michael Miller & Daniel Baier
Cedar Rapids, IA

Ponce de Limón

shot Captain Morgan
shot Bacardi Limón
splash cola

Michael Miller & Daniel Baier
Cedar Rapids, IA

Popper

1 part Cuervo tequila
1 part champagne

Layer in rocks glass. Cover the shot and slam it (gently) on the table. Drink it while it fizzes over. Use a very durable glass.

Popsicle

2 parts Boggs cranberry liqueur
2 parts Frangelico
1 part pineapple juice

Shake with ice and strain.

Portofino

1 shot Tuaca, chilled
Angostura bitters
lime and sugar

Face west (towards the ocean). Take a wedge of lime between your middle finger and thumb. Put two drops of Angostura bitters on the lime. No more, no less. Sprinkle 1/4 packet of sugar on the lime. No more, no less. Put the lime in your mouth. Remove the lime from your mouth and drink the shot.

Pot 'O Gold

2/3 oz. Goldschlager cinnamon schnapps
1/2 oz. Baileys Irish Cream

Build.

Prairie Fire

1 1/2 oz. Cuervo Gold tequila
dash Tabasco

Fill shot glass with chilled Cuervo Gold tequila. Add a dash of Tabasco.

Pretty in Pink

3/4 oz. Myers's Original dark rum
3/4 oz. crème de noyaux
1/2 oz. cream

Shake with ice and strain.

Pumpkin Pie

1 part Absolut vodka
1 part apple juice
1 dash cinnamon

Shake with ice and strain.

Pumpkin Smasher

1/2 oz. vodka
1/2 oz. Tuaca
1/4 oz. Hot Damn cinnamon schnapps
1/2 oz. peach schnapps
3 parts orange juice

Ken Hood
Port Arthur, TX

255

Puppy's Nose

1/2 oz. Kahlúa
1/2 oz. Tia Maria
1/2 oz. Rumple Minze peppermint
  schnapps
1/4 oz. Baileys Irish Cream

Shake with ice and strain.

Purple Haze

3/4 oz. Chambord
3/4 oz. Stolichnaya vodka
1/2 oz. cranberry juice or sour mix

Shake with ice and strain.

Purple Heart

1 part Absolut Kurant vodka
1 part Chambord
1 part cranberry juice

Shake with ice and strain.

Purple Hooter

3/4 oz. Finlandia vodka
3/4 oz. Chambord
1/2 oz. Rose's sweet & sour

Shake with ice and strain.

Purple Hooter #2

1/2 oz. Chambord
1 oz. vodka
1/2 oz. cranberry juice

Shake with ice and strain.

Purple Nurple

1/2 oz. tequila
splash Tabasco
1/4 oz. Hiram Walker blue curacao
1/4 oz. Hiram Walker sloe gin

Shake with ice and strain.

Purple Orchid

1/2 oz. white crème de cacao
1 oz. blackberry brandy
1/2 oz. cream

Shake with ice and strain.

Purple Panther

1 1/4 oz. Finlandia cranberry vodka
splash blue curacao

Shake with ice and strain.

Purple Passion

1 1/2 oz. Finlandia cranberry vodka
1/2 oz. Chambord

Shake with ice and strain.

Purple Peaches

1 oz. Stoli Persik
1/2 oz. peach schnapps
1/2 oz. Chambord

Jennifer Porter
Mt. Shasta, CA

Purple Perfection

1/2 oz. Chambord
1/2 oz. Absolut Citron
splash orange juice
splash pineapple juice
splash ginger ale

Patrick Billerman
Sea Girt, NJ

258

Purple Pirate

1/2 oz. Captain Morgan spiced rum
1/2 oz. Chambord
splash 7-Up

John Doyle
Philadelphia, PA

Purple Rain

1 splash blue curacao
1 1/2 oz. vodka
3/4 oz. cranberry juice

Shake with ice and strain.

Quick Silver

1/3 oz. white crème de cacao
1/3 oz. peppermint schnapps
1/3 oz. tequila

Quickie

1/2 oz. Hiram Walker crème de banana
1/2 oz. Hiram Walker blackberry brandy
1/2 oz. Carolans Irish Cream

Build.

259

Racer's Edge

1 oz. Bacardi light rum
1/4 oz. Hiram Walker crème de menthe
grapefruit juice

Shake with ice and strain.

Raggedy Andy

1 oz. Mozart chocolate liqueur
1/2 oz. crème de banana
1 oz. cream

Shake with ice and strain.

Raggedy Ann

1 oz. Mozart chocolate liqueur
1/2 oz. peppermint schnapps
1 oz. cream

Shake with ice and strain.

Raider

1/3 oz. Drambuie
1/3 oz. Baileys Irish Cream
1/3 oz. Grand Marnier
1/3 oz. Kahlúa

Rainbow

1/2 oz. crème de noyaux
1/2 oz. Midori melon liqueur
1/2 oz. white crème de cacao

Build.

Raspberry Brownie

3/4 oz. Chambord
3/4 oz. Kahlúa
float cream or milk

Raspberry Cheesecake

3/4 oz. Chambord
3/4 oz. Baileys Irish Cream
1/2 oz. cream

Build.

Raspberry Kiss

1 oz. Chambord
1/2 oz. Kahlúa
1 oz. cream

Shake with ice and strain.

Raspberry Screamer

1 oz. Chambord
1 oz. Absolut vodka
1 oz. pineapple juice

Shake with ice and strain.

Raspberry Shooter

1/3 Absolut vodka
2/3 Chambord
1 splash orange juice

Shake with ice and strain.

Raspberry Shortcake

1 oz. Chambord
1 oz. Baileys Irish Cream

Build.

Rastini

3/4 oz. Smirnoff vodka
3/4 oz. Chambord
splash Rose's sweet & sour
splash 7-Up

Shake with ice and strain. Top with 7-Up.

Rattlesnake

1 part Kahlúa
1 part Baileys Irish Cream
1 part dark crème de cacao

Add one part tequila and it's called a Mexican Rattlesnake. Build.

Rattlesnake #2

2/3 Yukon Jack
1/3 cherry brandy
1 splash sour mix

Shake with ice and strain.

Raven Shooter

1 oz. Malibu rum
1/2 oz. vodka
1/2 oz. pineapple juice
1/2 oz. cranberry juice

Shake with ice and strain.

Razor

3/4 oz. Bacardi 151 rum
3/4 oz. Disaronno amaretto
3/4 oz. Rumple Minze peppermint schnapps

Shake with ice and strain.

Real Gold

1 part Stolichnaya vodka
1 part Goldschlager cinnamon schnapps

Build.

Red & White

1 part Schladerer Himbeergeist
1 part Schladerer Himbeer liqueur
1 raspberry

Layer in pony glass. Raspberry floats in the middle.

Red Baron

1 1/2 oz. Absolut Kurant
splash vodka
splash cranberry juice

Build.

Red Bird Special

1 shot Absolut vodka
3 splashes tomato juice

Build.

264

Red Death

1/2 oz. Southern Comfort
1/2 oz. Disaronno amaretto
1/2 oz. sloe gin
2 splashes orange juice

Shake with ice and strain.

Red Devil

1/2 oz. Absolut vodka
1/2 oz. Bacardi light rum
1/4 oz. Southern Comfort
1/4 oz. Disaronno amaretto
1/4 oz. crème de cassis
1/2 splash sour mix

Shake with ice and serve.

Red Hot

1 1/4 oz. cinnamon schnapps
few drops Tabasco sauce

Build.

Red Hot #2

1/2 oz. Goldschlager cinnamon schnapps
1 oz. Stolichnaya vodka
dash Tabasco

Build.

Red Lobster

1/2 oz. Chambord
1/2 oz. Crown Royal
1/2 oz. amaretto
splash cranberry juice

Build.

Darek Dohy
Hard Rock Café
San Diego, CA

Red October

1 oz. Stolichnaya vodka
1/2 oz. Midori melon liqueur
1/2 oz. sloe gin
1/2 oz. orange juice
splash sour mix

Chill over ice and strain into shot glass.

David Whynot
Gillary's
Bristol, RI

Red Panties

1 oz. peach schnapps
1 oz. Smirnoff vodka
1/2 oz. grenadine
2 oz. orange juice

Shake with ice and strain.

Red Rum

1/2 oz. Southern Comfort
splash Jack Daniel's
1/2 oz. Myers's Original dark rum
cranberry juice
splash grenadine

Shake with ice and strain. Take one sip, spell the name backwards, and the rest is self-explanatory.

Stacey Wilson
G & M's Restaurant
Baltimore, MD

Red Russian

1 oz. Stolichnaya vodka
1/2 oz. pineapple juice
1/2 oz. grapefruit juice
float grenadine

Shake with ice and strain. Float dash grenadine.

Red Snapper

1/2 oz. amaretto
1/2 oz. Crown Royal
1/2 oz. cranberry juice

Build.

Red Whistle

1 1/4 oz. Finlandia cranberry vodka
1/8 oz. Rumple Minze peppermint schnapps
1/4 oz. Cointreau

Build. Serve in a test tube.

Red-Eyed Smiley Face

1/2 oz. Absolut Citron
1/2 oz. Tuaca
1/4 oz. Chambord
1/2 oz. sweet & sour mix
splash 7-Up

Regmeister

3/4 oz. Southern Comfort
3/4 oz. crème de noyaux
1/2 oz. 7-Up

Build. Top with 7-Up.

Revolution

1 oz. ouzo
1/2 oz. Liquore Galliano
1 dash grenadine

Layer in the following order: grenadine, ouzo, Galliano.

269

Rhett Butler

1 oz. Southern Comfort
1/2 oz. triple sec
1/2 splash Rose's lime juice
1/2 splash sour mix

Shake with ice and strain.

Rigor Mortis

1/4 oz. amaretto
1 oz. vodka
1/2 oz. orange juice
1/2 oz. pineapple juice

Shake with ice and strain.

Rimanto Chill

Rimanto Potato vodka, chilled

Enjoy straight up.

River Runner

1 1/2 oz. Absolut Kurant vodka
1/4 oz. blue curacao
1/4 oz. pineapple juice
1/4 oz. sour mix

Shake with ice and strain.

Roadrunner

1/2 oz. Kahlúa
1/2 oz. Grand Marnier

Shake with ice and strain.

Rock Lobster

1 part white crème de cacao
1 part Baileys Irish Cream
1 splash Goldschlager cinnamon schnapps

Build.

Rocket Fuel

3/4 oz. Rumple Minze peppermint schnapps
1/2 oz. Bacardi 151 rum

Build.

Rocky Mountain

1 oz. Southern Comfort
1 oz. Disaronno amaretto
1/2 oz. lime juice

Shake with ice and strain.

Rocky Road

1/2 oz. Disaronno amaretto
1/2 oz. Baileys Irish Cream
1/2 oz. Wild Turkey

Combine amaretto and Baileys with ice.
Shake and strain. Float Wild Turkey.

Roman Candle

1 oz. anisette
1/2 oz. Liquore Galliano
1/2 oz. orange juice
dash grenadine

Shake with ice and strain.

Roman Martini

1/2 oz. Romana sambuca
1 1/2 oz. Bombay gin

Shake with ice and strain.

Roo-Kon

3/4 oz. Yukon Jack
1/4 oz. root beer schnapps

Build.

John Fazio
Pittsburgh, PA

Root Beer Float

2 parts DeKuyper Old Tavern root beer
   schnapps
1 part Baileys Irish Cream

Make in a test tube. Fill each tube 3/4 with
root beer schnapps and top with Baileys.
Garnish tube with a cherry.

Root Beer Float #2

3/4 oz. Liquore Galliano
3/4 oz. Kahlúa
1 splash cola
1 splash half & half

Stir with ice and strain.

273

Root Beer Shooter

1 oz. Kahlúa
1/2 oz. Liquore Galliano
cola

Shake with ice and strain. Top with cola.

Root Canal

Liquore Galliano
root beer schnapps

Equal parts.

Root Canal #2

3/4 oz. root beer schnapps
3/4 oz. Nassau Royale

Bill Bona
Celebration, FL

Ruby Ridge

1 oz. Southern Comfort 101
1/2 oz. amaretto
1/2 oz. sweet & sour
splash cranberry juice and 7-Up

Brian Psencik
Austin, TX

Ruby Slippers

1 part Finlandia cranberry vodka
1 part Goldschlager cinnamon schnapps

Build.

Rum Runner

1 part Bacardi dark rum
1 part Bacardi light rum
1 part blackberry brandy
1 part crème de banana
1 part Malibu

Add to taste—orange juice, sour mix, and a dash of grenadine. Shake with ice and strain.

Rumple Meister

1/2 oz. Rumple Minze peppermint schnapps
1/2 oz. Jagermeister

Serve chilled.

Rumpled Rose

3/4 shot Rumple Minze, chilled
1/2 shot Tequila Rose, chilled

Layer in frozen shot glass.

275

Rush Hour

1/3 oz. Kahlúa
1/3 oz. sambuca
1/3 oz. Baileys Irish Cream

Russian Defect

1 oz. Stolichnaya vodka
1/2 oz. Rumple Minze peppermint schnapps

Build.

Russian Quaalude

1/3 shot Stolichnaya vodka
1/3 shot Frangelico
1/3 shot Baileys Irish Cream

Shake with ice and strain.

Russian Roulette

1/2 oz. Stolichnaya, chilled
1/2 oz. Liquore Galliano, chilled
splash Bacardi 151

Place a piece of round-cut, sugared lemon
on shot glass. Pour splash Bacardi 151, bite
lemon, and do shot.

Rusted Throat

1/2 oz. DeKuyper Key Largo schnapps
1/2 oz. Bacardi 151 rum
1/2 oz. Bacardi light rum
1/2 oz. Tropicana orange juice

Shake with ice and strain.

Rory L. Chatman
Norfolk, VA

Rusty Nail Shooter

1 part Drambuie liqueur
1 part J&B scotch

Build.

S.O.B.

3/4 oz. Southern Comfort
1/2 oz. Cointreau
1 lemon wedge

Shake with ice and strain. Suck lemon
wedge then shoot.

Safe Sex on the Beach

3/4 oz. Chambord
3/4 oz. peach schnapps
1 oz. orange juice

Shake with ice and strain.

Saint Moritz

1 1/4 oz. Chambord
cream

Pour liqueur into glass. Float cream.

Salmon Run

1 oz. Jose Cuervo tequila
1 oz. tomato juice
1 oz. orange juice

Three consecutive shots in three glasses.

Dennis (DJ) Johnson
Sheridan, WY

Sambuca

1 oz. sambuca
3 coffee beans

Sambuca Slide

1 oz. Romana sambuca
1/2 oz. Stolichnaya vodka
1/2 oz. light cream

Shake with ice and strain.

Sambuca Surprise

1/2 oz. Romana sambuca
1/2 oz. white crème de menthe
1/2 oz. white crème de cacao

Build.

Sand in Your Butt

1 part Southern Comfort
1 part Midori melon liqueur
2 parts pineapple juice

Shake with ice and strain.

Sand Slide

1/2 oz. Carolans Irish Cream
1/2 oz. Kahlúa
1/2 oz. Frïs vodka

Shake with ice and strain.

Sandblaster

1/2 oz. Jagermeister
1/4 oz. CJ Wray dry rum
1/2 oz. cola

Squeeze lime wedge. Build.

Json Nakagawa
Tony Roma's
Westridge, HI

Saratoga Trunk

1 oz. Tia Maria
1 oz. Tuaca
1/2 oz. Hiram Walker cinnamon schnapps

Layer ingredients in the following order: Tia Maria, Tuaca, float cinnamon schnapps.

Scarlett O'Hara Shooter

1 oz. Southern Comfort
1/2 splash grenadine
1 splash sour mix

Shake with ice and strain.

Scooter

1 oz. Disaronno amaretto
1/2 oz. brandy
1 oz. light cream

Shake with ice and strain into cordial glass.

Scorpion

1/2 oz. vodka
1 oz. blackberry brandy

Shake with ice and strain.

Screamin' Coyote

1 part Firewater
1 part Goldschlager cinnamon schnapps
1 part Rumple Minze peppermint schnapps

Serve in a double shot glass.

Ivan
Arlington Hotel
Kane, PA

Screaming Cranapple Shooter

1 oz. Absolut vodka
1 oz. apple schnapps
1 splash cranberry juice

Shake with ice and strain.

Screaming Green Monster

1/2 oz. Malibu rum
1/2 oz. Midori
1/2 oz. Bacardi 151
splash pineapple juice
splash 7-Up

Michael Williams
Huntington Beach, CA

Screaming Multiple Orgasm

1/4 oz. Liquore Galliano
1/2 oz. Cointreau
1/2 oz. Baileys Irish Cream
1/2 oz. cream

Shake with ice and strain.

Screaming Orgasm

1/2 oz. Kahlúa
1/2 oz. Disaronno amaretto
1/2 oz. Baileys Irish Cream
1/4 oz. Absolut vodka

Build.

Screaming Orgasm #2

1/2 oz. Frïs vodka
1/2 oz. Baileys Irish Cream
1/2 oz. Kahlúa
1/2 oz. cream

Shake with ice and strain.

Screaming Orgasm #3

1/2 oz. Stolichnaya vodka
1/4 oz. Southern Comfort
1/4 oz. Cuervo tequila
1/2 oz. Kahlúa
1/2 oz. cream

Shake with ice and strain.

Screaming Orgasm against the Wall

1/4 oz. Disaronno amaretto
1/4 oz. Baileys Irish Cream
1/4 oz. banana liqueur
1/4 oz. Liquore Galliano
1/4 oz. Kahlúa
1/4 oz. Finlandia vodka
1/4 oz. cream

Shake with ice and strain.

Scud Patriot

Needed: 1 rocks glass, 1 shooter glass

"Scud"

To skim along swiftly and easily.
1/4 shot Crown Royal
1/2 shot peach schnapps
1 oz. sweet & sour mix
splash 7-Up

Shake, strain, serve in rocks glass.

"Patriot"

One who loves, supports, and defends one's country.
1/2 shot Crown Royal
splash 7-Up

Serve in shooter glass. To drink, slam "Scud," then slam "Patriot."

Annemarie Boese
Dallas, TX

Second Childhood

1/2 oz. Rumple Minze peppermint schnapps
1/2 oz. Jagermeister
1/2 oz. Frïs vodka

Build.

Separator

3/4 oz. Kahlúa
3/4 oz. brandy
1/2 oz. cream

Build.

Seven Forty-Seven (747)

1 part Kahlúa
1 part Baileys Irish Cream
1 part Frangelico

Shake with ice and strain.

Sex in the Parking Lot

1/2 oz. Chambord
1/2 oz. Smirnoff vodka
1/2 oz. apple schnapps

Shake with ice and strain.

Sex on the Beach

1/2 oz. Chambord
1/2 oz. Midori melon liqueur
1/2 oz. Absolut vodka
pineapple juice

Shake with ice and strain.

Sex on the Beach #2

3/4 oz. Absolut vodka
3/4 oz. peach schnapps
1/4 oz. cranberry juice
1/4 oz. orange juice
3/4 oz. Midori melon liqueur

Shake with ice and strain.

Sex on the Beach #3

3/4 oz. Chambord
1/2 oz. pineapple juice

Shake with ice and strain.

Sex on the Beach #4

1 part Southern Comfort
1 part peach schnapps
1 part Chambord
2 parts cranberry juice
2 parts pineapple juice

For "Better Sex" try substituting DeKuyper Key Largo schnapps for peach. Shake with ice and strain.

Sex on the Beach (Southern Style)

1/2 oz. peach schnapps
1/2 oz. apple schnapps
1/2 oz. cranberry juice
1/2 oz. pineapple juice

Shake with ice and strain.

Sex on the Lake

3/4 oz. crème de banana
3/4 oz. dark crème de cacao
dash Bacardi light rum
1/2 oz. cream

Shake with ice and strain.

Sex on the Pool Table

1/2 oz. blueberry schnapps
1/2 oz. Midori melon liqueur
1/2 oz. Finlandia vodka
1/2 oz. orange juice
1/2 oz. pineapple juice

Shake with ice and strain.

Sex on the Sidewalk

3/4 oz. Midori melon liqueur
3/4 oz. Chambord
1/2 oz. cranberry juice

Shake with ice and strain.

Sex Up against the Wall

Absolut Kurant vodka
pineapple juice
cranberry juice
sour mix

Equal parts. Shake with ice and strain.

Sex with the Captain

1/2 oz. amaretto
1/2 oz. Captain Morgan spiced rum
1/2 oz. peach schnapps
splash cranberry juice
splash orange juice

Shake with ice and strain.

Sex, Lies, and Video Poker

1/2 oz. Captain Morgan spiced rum
1/2 oz. amaretto
1/2 oz. Southern Comfort
1/2 oz. orange juice
1/2 oz. pineapple juice
1/2 oz. cranberry juice
1/2 oz. grenadine

Shake with ice and strain into shot glass.
Makes four.

John Dugas, Jr.
J&K Bar
New Orleans, LA

Sexy Rose

1/2 Tequila Rose
1/2 Original Bartenders Hot Sex

Jeff Bowen
Monroe, WI

Shark Bite Shooter

1 part Myers's Original dark rum
2 parts orange juice
1 splash grenadine

Shake with ice and strain.

289

Sharpshooter

1 oz. ouzo
1 oz. vodka
dash Tabasco

Shazam

1/2 oz. Cuervo Gold tequila
1/2 oz. Chambord
1/2 oz. DeKuyper Peachtree schnapps
4 oz. sour mix
splash beer

Clair Beshears
Milford, MA

Shipwreck

1 oz. Crown Royal
1/4 oz. crème de banana
1/4 oz. triple sec
1/4 oz. sweet & sour mix
1/4 oz. cranberry juice

Shake with ice and strain.

Shock Treatment

1 oz. Grand Marnier
1 oz. Tia Maria

Build.

Shogun Shooter

1/2 oz. Midori melon liqueur
1 1/4 oz. Frïs vodka

Shake with ice and strain.

Shot of C

1 1/2 oz. Cruzan orange tropical–flavored
   rum

Greg Czarnecki
West Palm Beach, FL

Shot of Ed

1 oz. 151 Bacardi rum
1/2 oz. Jagermeister
1/2 oz. Rumple Minze

Sean Meche, Joey Foret, and Kris Heggelund
Lafayette, LA

Shot-O-Happiness

1/4 oz. Goldschlager
1/2 oz. Chambord
splash 7-Up
Equal parts:
  sweet & sour
  pineapple juice

Juan Sandoval
San Antonio, TX

Siberian Express

Equal parts:
  Kahlúa
  Dr. McGuillicuddy's Menthol schnapps
  Smirnoff vodka
  half & half

Debbie Burt
Winter, WI

Siberian Gold

1 part Stolichnaya vodka
1 part Goldschlager cinnamon schnapps
splash blue curacao

Shake with ice and strain.

Chris "Skippy" Jones & Gerald "I'm not Randy"
  Kirkman
Bananas
Beaufort, SC

Siberian Toolkit

1 oz. Stolichnaya vodka
1/4 oz. Seagram's V.O.
1/4 oz. Kahlúa
1/4 oz. Baileys Irish Cream

Shake with ice and strain.

Sicilian Kiss

1 part Southern Comfort
1 part Disaronno amaretto
3 parts orange juice
1 dash grenadine

Build. Add the grenadine on top to make a sunset effect.

Silk Panties

1 part Stolichnaya vodka
1 part DeKuyper Peachtree schnapps

Build.

Silver Bullet

1/2 oz. green crème de menthe
1/2 oz. tequila

Silver Spider

1/2 oz. Smirnoff vodka
1/2 oz. Bacardi rum
1/4 oz. Cointreau
1/2 oz. white crème de menthe

Stir with ice and strain.

Silver Thread

1/3 oz. crème de banana
1/3 oz. peppermint schnapps
1/3 oz. Baileys Irish Cream

Simply Bonkers

1 oz. Chambord
1/2 oz. Bacardi rum
1/2 oz. cream

Shake with ice and strain.

Sinful Apple

1 part Rimanto Potato vodka
3/4 part Schoenauer Apfel schnapps

Shake and serve.

Sinfully Hot

3/4 oz. tequila
splash Tabasco
1/4 oz. Hiram Walker cinnamon schnapps

Shake with ice and strain.

Sit Down & Shut Up

1/3 oz. blackberry brandy
1/3 oz. Southern Comfort
1/3 oz. Rumple Minze peppermint schnapps

Shake with ice and strain.

Skandia-Iceberg

Equal parts:
  Klar Eis peppermint schnapps
  Frïs vodka Skandia

Skid Mark

3/4 oz. Kahlúa
3/4 oz. Baileys Irish Cream
3/4 oz. Guinness

Donna Collins
Ocean City, MD

Skinny Mulligan

1/3 oz. crème de banana
1/3 oz. advocaat
1/3 oz. sloe gin

Skip and Go Naked

1 part Beefeater gin
2 parts sour mix
1 splash beer

Stir slowly with ice and strain.

Slam Dunk Shooter

1 oz. Monte Alban tequila
1 splash Rose's lime juice
1 splash club soda

Serve in pony or cordial glass. Cover glass
with hand and rap on table.

Slammer

1 oz. amaretto
1 oz. 7-Up

Cover with napkin and slam on bar. Drink
while fizzing.

Slice of Apple Pie

1 1/4 oz. Smirnoff vodka
1/2 oz. apple juice

Sprinkle with cinnamon. Build.

Slickie Ricky

1 oz. watermelon schnapps
1/2 oz. Original Bartenders Hot Sex
squirt whipped cream

Suck down.

Gina Geremia
New Haven, CT

Slickster

1/2 oz. Southern Comfort
1/4 oz. peach schnapps
1 oz. cranberry juice
1/4 oz. 7-Up

Stir with ice and strain.

Slimeball

1/2 cup Midori melon liqueur
1/2 cup Smirnoff vodka
1 cup boiling water
lime Jell-O brand gelatin

Add Midori and boiling water to lime Jell-O.
Add vodka. Chill to set. Serve in paper souf-
flé cups. (The Slimeball is a variation of the
Jell-O shot.)

Slippery Baileys

1/2 oz. Baileys Irish Cream
1/2 oz. Kahlúa
1/2 oz. crème de banana

Layer Kahlúa, then crème de banana, then
Baileys in a shot glass.

Slippery Chicken

Carolans Irish Cream
crème de banana
Grand Marnier

Equal parts.

Slippery Lips

1 oz. Absolut vodka
1/2 oz. Chambord
1/2 oz. triple sec
1/2 oz. cranberry juice
1/2 oz. orange juice
1/2 oz. sour mix

Strain into shot glass. Serves four.

David Quidk
Luke's Sports Spectacular
Milwaukee, WI

Slippery Nipple

2/3 oz. Romana sambuca
1/3 oz. Baileys Irish Cream
drop grenadine

Build. Add 1 drop grenadine in center.

Slippery Nipple #2

1/3 oz. anisette
1/3 oz. peppermint schnapps
1/3 oz. Baileys Irish Cream

Slippery Saddle

1/2 oz. Finlandia vodka
1/2 oz. Licor 43
1/2 oz. orange juice
1/2 oz. lemon juice

Shake with ice and strain.

Sloe Slop

1/4 oz. 7-Up
1/2 oz. sloe gin
1 oz. Stolichnaya vodka

Shake with ice and strain. Top with 7-Up.

Smelly Cat

1 oz. Bacardi Limón
1/2 oz. peach schnapps
splash cranberry juice

Lisa S. Acosta
East Rutherford, NJ

Smiles

1/2 oz. Canadian Club
1/2 oz. Hiram Walker peppermint schnapps
1/2 oz. Hiram Walker amaretto

Shake with ice and strain.

Smokey Joe

1 shot Tia Maria
1 shot Opal Nera

Marion DeFazio
Dickson City, PA

Smoot and Sweet

3/4 oz. blackberry liqueur
3/4 oz. amaretto
1/2 oz. pineapple juice

Shake with ice and strain.

Snake Bite

2 parts Yukon Jack
1 part Rose's lime juice

Shake with ice and strain.

Snake Bite #2

1 oz. Jack Daniel's
1/2 oz. Rumple Minze peppermint schnapps

Build.

Snake Bite #3

Canadian Club
Hiram Walker peppermint schnapps

Equal parts.

Snap Dragon

1/2 oz. Crown Royal
1/2 oz. amaretto
1/4 oz. cranberry juice
splash orange juice

Gina Geremia
New Haven, CT

Sneakers

3/4 oz. amaretto
1/2 oz. vodka
3/4 oz. pineapple juice

Shake with ice and strain.

Sneeker

1/2 oz. Chambord
1/2 oz. Malibu rum
1/2 oz. Bacardi 151
1/2 oz. Midori
splash cranberry juice and 7-Up

Snickers

1/2 oz. Baileys Irish Cream
1/2 oz. dark crème de cacao
1/2 oz. Frangelico

Shake with ice and strain.

Snow Ball

1 oz. Bacardi rum
1/2 oz. Coco Lopéz cream of coconut
1/2 oz. pineapple juice

Blend with ice and serve.

Snow Cap

1/2 oz. Sauza tequila
1/2 oz. Baileys Irish Cream

Build tequila and Baileys in a shot glass.

Snow Drop

1/4 oz. Liquore Galliano
1/4 oz. Stolichnaya vodka
1/4 oz. Cointreau
1/4 oz. white crème de cacao
1 oz. cream

Shake with ice and strain.

Snow Melter

3/4 oz. Romana sambuca
1/2 oz. Stubbs rum
1/2 oz. white crème de cacao

Pour into shot glass.

Snowflake

1 part Hiram Walker peppermint schnapps
1 part Beefeater gin

Build.

Snowshoe

1 1/2 oz. Southern Comfort
1 oz. Rumple Minze peppermint schnapps

Build.

So Co Slammer

1 part Southern Comfort
2 parts cola

Build.

Soi Sant Neuf Volcano

1 1/2 oz. Soi Sant Neuf

Shoot the Soi Sant Neuf. Follow with a beer chaser.

Son of a Beach

1 oz. Fris vodka
3/4 oz. Hiram Walker blue curacao
1 oz. 7-Up

Shake with ice and strain. Top with 7-Up.

Sorry Bastard

1 part Jagermeister
1 part Cuervo tequila

Build.

Sour Apple

3/4 oz. Southern Comfort
3/4 oz. Midori melon liqueur
dash sour mix

Shake with ice and strain.

Sour Apple Rancher

3/4 oz. Midori
3/4 oz. Southern Comfort

Fill with Daily's Sweet & Sour Mix.

Vonnie Miller
Greensburg, PA

Sour Grapes

1/2 oz. Finlandia vodka
1/2 oz. Chambord
1/2 oz. sour mix

Shake with ice and strain.

Sour Lemon

1 oz. Fris vodka
dash Rose's lime juice
1 1/2 oz. sweet & sour mix

Shake with ice and strain.

South of the Border Root Beer

1/2 oz. tequila
splash Tabasco
1/2 oz. Hiram Walker root beer schnapps

Shake with ice and strain.

Southern Belle

3/4 oz. Southern Comfort
3/4 oz. Baileys Irish Cream

Shake with ice and strain.

Spanish Fly

1 oz. Sauza Gold tequila
1/2 oz. Liquore Galliano
1/2 oz. orange juice

Shake with ice and strain.

Spanish Moss

1/2 oz. Cuervo tequila
3/4 oz. Kahlúa
1/2 oz. green crème de menthe

Shake with ice and strain.

Sparkling Raspberry

1/2 oz. Chambord
1 1/2 oz. champagne

Build.

Spasm

1 1/2 oz. Disaronno amaretto
1/2 oz. Kahlúa
1/2 oz. Baileys Irish Cream

Build.

Specimen

1 oz. Finlandia vodka, chilled
1/2 oz. pineapple juice

Serve in test tube.

Speed Ball

Jagermeister
Goldschlager cinnamon schnapps
Rumple Minze peppermint schnapps

Equal parts. Build.
"If this doesn't get you moving, nothing will."

Jimmy Oppel
Bobby Valentine's Sport Gallery Café
Middletown, RI

Spider Bite

1/2 oz. anisette
1/2 oz. tequila

Spike

1 part Cuervo tequila
1 part grapefruit juice

Build.

Squirrels Fantasy

1 oz. amaretto
1/2 oz. white crème de noyaux
1/2 oz. Frangelico
splash club soda

Build. Top with club soda.

Pat Ensten
Brannigans Bar and Grill
Stillwater, OK

Stalactite

1 1/8 oz. Romana sambuca
1/4 oz. Baileys Irish Cream
1/4 oz. Chambord

Pour sambuca into cordial glass. Float Baileys on top. Pour Chambord drop by drop as top layer. The Chambord will pull the Baileys through the sambuca and will settle on the bottom.

Star Wars

1 oz. Southern Comfort
1/2 oz. Grand Marnier
1/2 oz. orange juice

Shake with ice and strain.

Star Wars #2

1/3 sloe gin
1/3 Grand Marnier
1/3 orange juice

Shake with ice and strain.

Starburst

3/4 oz. Malibu
1/2 oz. Finlandia vodka
1/4 oz. Chambord
1/2 oz. pineapple juice
1/2 oz. cranberry juice

Shake with ice and strain.

Stars and Stripes

1/3 oz. grenadine
1/3 oz. heavy cream
1/3 oz. blue curacao

Layer in order in cordial glass.

Stealth Bomber

1/2 oz. Kahlúa
1/2 oz. crème de banana
1/2 oz. Baileys Irish Cream
1/2 oz. Grand Marnier

Shake with ice and strain.

Steamboat Special

1/4 oz. Grand Marnier
1 oz. J&B scotch

Float Grand Marnier and serve.

Stiff Richard

Damiana Mexican liqueur
Captain Morgan spiced rum
pineapple juice

Equal parts. Shake and strain over ice, pour
into shot glass.

Vance Brown & Mark Todd
Diamond Lil's
Eureka Springs, AR

Stiffed Again

1 1/2 oz. B&B brandy, chilled
splash club soda

Build.

Stiletto Shooter

1/3 oz. Kahlúa
1/3 oz. peppermint schnapps
1/3 oz. tequila

Stinger Shooter

2/3 oz. brandy
1/3 oz. white crème de menthe

Shake with ice and strain.

Stingray

1 1/4 oz. Finlandia cranberry vodka
1/4 oz. white crème de menthe

Shake with ice and strain.

Stinky Pinky

3/4 oz. Stoli Persik vodka
3/4 oz. Stoli Ohranj vodka
1/2 oz. Cointreau
1/2 oz. cranberry juice
1/2 oz. sweet & sour mix

Shake with ice.

Stoli Buster

2/3 oz. Stolichnaya vodka
2/3 oz. Baileys Irish Cream

Stir and strain.

Stoli Ohranj Drop

1 1/4 oz. Stolichnaya Ohranj vodka

Serve with an orange wedge coated in sugar. Shoot the Ohranj, then eat the sugar-coated orange wedge.

Stony

Enjoy icy Echt Stonsdorfer shots straight up.

Stop and Go

1 oz. Finlandia cranberry vodka
1/2 oz. Midori melon liqueur
1/8 oz. triple sec

Chill ingredients until ice cold. Rim shot glass with sugar. Pour ingredients slowly in stated order over back of spoon into glass.

Stop and Go Naked

1/4 oz. Absolut vodka
1/4 oz. Tangueray gin
1/4 oz. Bacardi rum
1/4 oz. Cuervo tequila
1/2 oz. triple sec
1/2 oz. lemon juice

Shake with ice and strain. Add dash of beer on top.

Storm Cloud

1 oz. Disaronno amaretto
1/3 oz. Bacardi 151 rum
dash half & half

Shake with ice and strain.

Stormy

3/4 oz. Opal Nera black sambuca
1/2 oz. Grand Marnier
1/2 oz. cream

Shake with ice and strain.

Stranded in Tijuana

1/4 sloe gin
1/4 Jose Cuervo Especial
1/4 Green Chartreuse
1/4 Bacardi 151 rum

Shake with ice and strain.

Strawberry Blonde

3/4 oz. strawberry schnapps
3/4 oz. Baileys Irish Cream

Build.

Strawberry Quick with a Kick

1 oz. Tequila Rose
1 oz. Chambord
1/2 oz. Stoli Razberi vodka

Mike Sicliano
Saratoga Springs, NY

316

Strip and Go Naked

1/2 oz. Bacardi 151 rum
1/2 oz. Stolichnaya vodka
1/4 oz. triple sec
1/4 oz. cherry brandy
1/2 oz. sour mix

Shake with ice and strain.

Suicide Blonde

1 oz. Finlandia vodka
1/2 oz. pineapple juice
dash triple sec
dash lime juice

Shake with ice and strain.

Sunkist

1 1/4 oz. Stolichnaya Ohranj vodka
1/4 oz. Chambord

Steve Kellard
Bethlehem, PA

Sunset

3/4 oz. Absolut vodka
dash orange juice
1/2 oz. grenadine
dash 7-Up

Shake with ice and strain, dash 7-Up.

Sunset at the Beach

1 1/4 oz. Finlandia cranberry vodka
1/4 oz. raspberry liqueur
1/4 oz. Midori melon liqueur
2 oz. pineapple juice

Shake with ice and strain.

Suntan Lotion

Equal parts, chilled:
  Baileys Irish Cream
  Parrot Bay rum

Mix over ice, strain into a shot glass.

Denise DeSena
Bay Shore, NY

Super Screw or F.S.

1 1/4 oz. Stolichnaya vodka
1/4 oz. orange juice

Top with club soda.

Ryan Peters
Wall, NJ

Supermodel Shot

1 1/2 oz. Bacardi Limón
1/2 oz. Midori
1/2 oz. blue curacao

Bacardi-Martini USA, Inc.
Miami, FL

Surfers on Acid

3/4 oz. Jagermeister
1/2 oz. Malibu rum
splash pineapple juice

Debra Welch
New London, NH

Surfers on Acid #2

1/3 Jagermeister
1/3 Captain Morgan coconut rum
1/3 pineapple juice
dash grenadine

Build.

Swamp Water

3/4 oz. Green Chartreuse
3/4 oz. Cointreau
1/2 oz. pineapple juice

Shake with ice and strain.

Sweaty Irishman!

1/2 oz. Jameson Irish whiskey
1/2 oz. Hot Damn cinnamon schnapps
dash Tabasco

Angela Peyton
Alamosa, CO

Swedish Kiss

1 1/2 oz. Absolut Kurant vodka
splash Chambord

Build. Top with club soda.

Swedish Quaalude

1/3 oz. Absolut vodka
1/3 oz. Frangelico
1/3 oz. Baileys Irish Cream

Shake with ice and strain.

Sweet 'N Tart

1 1/2 oz. Absolut Citron
splash sweet & sour
splash 7-Up
1 tsp. sugar
twist lime and lemon

Makes two shots.

Orlando V. Villarreal, XBAR10DR
United States Marine Corps. USS
Comstock, Somewhere in the Western Pacific

Sweet Tooth

1 oz. vodka
1/4 oz. triple sec
1/4 oz. peach schnapps
splash cherry brandy
splash Rose's lime juice

Shake with ice and strain.

Sweetpea

1/3 Rumple Minze
1/3 buttershots schnapps
1/3 Baileys Irish Cream

Louie Andrakakos
College Park, MD

T.N.T. Cocktail

3/4 oz. Seagram's V.O.
3/4 oz. Hiram Walker anisette

Shake with ice and strain.

Tame a Monkey

1 part 99 Bananas
1/2 part Master of Mixers strawberry
  daiquiri mix
1 part pineapple juice
1 part orange juice
touch of grenadine

Doran Villnave
Massena, NY

Tart 'N Tangy

1 oz. Bacardi Limón
1 part sour mix
1 part cranberry juice
splash grenadine

Shake with ice and strain into a shot glass.

Alberto Escoffery
Amherst, MA

Taxicab

1/2 oz. Grand Marnier
1/2 oz. Absolut Citron
1/2 oz. DeKuyper Peachtree schnapps
1/2 oz. pineapple juice

James Montgomery
Houston, TX

TBF

1/2 oz. Tia Maria
1/2 oz. Baileys Irish Cream
1/2 oz. Frangelico

Robert Knapton/Guin Black
Las Vegas, NV

T-Bird

1 part Grand Marnier
1 part Hiram Walker amaretto
1 part Absolut vodka
2 1/2 oz. pineapple juice
splash cream (optional)

Shake with ice and strain.

Teddy Bear

1/2 oz. root bear schnapps
1 oz. vodka

Layer root beer schnapps and vodka in a shot glass.

Tequila Mockingbird Shooter

Swiss chocolate almond
amaretto
tequila

Tequila Popper

1 oz. tequila
1/2 oz. 7-Up

Pour tequila into a shot glass. Fill with 7-Up. Place a napkin over the top of the glass and bang the glass down onto the table. Drink immediately.

Tequila Shot

1 1/2 oz. tequila
1 pinch salt
1 lemon or lime wedge

A premium brand of tequila is recommended. Fill a shot glass with tequila (chilled, if desired). Put salt between thumb and index finger of left hand. While holding shot glass in the same hand, and the lemon or lime wedge in the other hand, lick the salt and quickly drink the shot of tequila. Suck the lemon or lime immediately afterward.

Tequila Sunrise Shooter

1 part tequila
2 parts orange juice
splash grenadine

Chill and strain. Drop the grenadine on the top to give it that sunrise look.

Tequini

1 1/2 oz. Sauza Conmemorativo tequila
1/4 oz. Martini & Rossi extra dry vermouth

Shake with ice and strain.

Terminator

1/2 oz. brandy
1/2 oz. Kahlúa
1/2 oz. Wild Turkey

Build.

Terminator #2

1/2 Jagermeister
1/2 Southern Comfort

Build.

Test Tube Baby

2 parts strawberry schnapps
1 part Baileys Irish Cream
1 small gummi bear

Fill a test tube 3/4 with chilled strawberry schnapps, then add chilled Baileys. Drop the gummi bear in the top and let it sink to the bottom.

Test Tube Baby #2

3/4 oz. amaretto
1/2 oz. Southern Comfort

Layer Southern Comfort on top of amaretto. Add 1 to 2 drops of cream to bottom of drink with a short straw.

Test Tube Baby #3

3/4 oz. amaretto
1/2 oz. tequila

Add 1 to 2 drops of cream to bottom of drink with a short straw.

The Astropop

3/4 oz. Yukon Jack, chilled
3/4 oz. Goldschlager, chilled
1/4 oz. Midori
1/4 oz. grenadine

Michael Kane
Santa Maria, CA

The Atomic Shot

1/2 oz. Goldschlager cinnamon schnapps
1/2 oz. Absolut Peppar vodka
1/2 oz. Jose Cuervo tequila
splash soda water

Build.

Stephan Porter
Lazy Armadillo
Woodsocket, RI

The Barney

1 oz. grape pucker
1/2 oz. triple sec
1 oz. Bacardi
splash 7-Up & sour mix

Mix with ice and strain into a shot glass.

Dave Isaacs
St. Cloud, MN

The Batman

Traditional B-52
In a shot glass place:
  1/3 Kahlúa
  1/3 Baileys Irish Cream
  1/3 Grand Marnier
In 16 oz. mixer or beverage glass place:
  1 oz. Bacardi rum
  Coke

Fill glass half full with ice. Drop shot of B-52 into rum and Coke and bamn! You have a Batman.

Brett Althoff
St. Louis Park, MN

The Berry Kix

1 1/4 oz. Absolut Kurant vodka
cranberry juice
sweet & sour mix

Equal parts of cranberry juice and sweet & sour mix. Shake with ice and strain.

The Blue Bayou

3/4 oz. Southern Comfort
3/4 oz. blue curacao
3/4 oz. pineapple juice

Shane Karlin
Campbell, CA

The Brigantine Greenhead

1 oz. Absolut vodka
1 oz. Southern Comfort
1 oz. tequila
splash green crème de menthe (just to color)

Gary R. Tracy, Sr.
Brigantine, NJ

The Butterfly

1 part Carolans Irish Cream
1 part Hiram Walker butterscotch schnapps

Build.

The Butterscotch Slide

1 oz. Baileys Irish Cream
1 oz. Kahlúa
1 oz. butterscotch schnapps
2 oz. milk

David Tothill
Lockport, NY

The Captain's Cream Soda Slammer

1 part Captain Morgan Original spiced
  rum
1 part lemon lime soda

Pour Captain Morgan rum in shot glass.
Top with soda. Cover top of glass with napkin. Slam down hard on counter; serve immediately.

The Devil You Don't Know

1/2 Jagermeister
1/2 Mozart chocolate liqueur

Build.

The Dirty Leprechaun

1/3 Jagermeister
1/3 Baileys Irish Cream
1/3 Midori melon liqueur

Build or shake with ice.

"The Don"

1/4 oz. dark crème de cacao
1/4 oz. white crème de cacao
1/4 oz. gin
1 oz. vodka

Layer in shot glass.

The Equalizer

1/2 oz. peach schnapps
3/4 oz. Jagermeister
1/2 oz. orange juice
1/2 oz. pineapple juice

Shake with ice and strain.

The Flame

1 1/4 oz. Absolut Peppar vodka
1/4 oz. Cherry Mariner

Build.

The Frazzle

1 oz. Baileys Irish Cream
1 oz. Captain Morgan spiced rum

Build. Serve in shot glass.

Sharon McHenry
Tommy's Mardi Gras
Stone Park, IL

The Fuzzy Monkey

1 oz. crème de banana
1/4 oz. peach schnapps
3/4 oz. orange juice

Shake with ice; strain into shooter glass.

Scott Swigart
East Village Grill and Bar
Raleigh, NC

The Manhattan Project

1/4 oz. amaretto
1/4 oz. peppermint schnapps
1/4 oz. Southern Comfort
1/4 oz. white tequila

Nick Vandenbroucke
San Diego, CA

The Neapolitan

Layer in shot glass:
   dark crème de cacao
   Dr. McGillicuddy's vanilla schnapps

Top with Tequila Rose.

Mickey Thornton
West Covina, CA

The Orangatang

Southern Comfort
Absolut vodka
Midori melon liqueur
orange juice

Equal parts. Blend and chill, serve in shot glass.

Kim
Tommy's Mardi Gras
Stone Park, IL

The Pernod Demon

1 1/2 oz. Pernod

A wedge of lemon coated with sugar and doused with Tabasco. Just suck the lemon and then shoot the Pernod.

The Runyan

1 part vodka
1 part Chambord
splash grape Kool-Aid

Build.

Joe Witters
Joe's Bar
Colorado Springs, CO

The Runyan #2

1 part vodka
1 part Chambord
splash sweet & sour

Charlene Witten
Colorado Springs, CO

The Screw

1 shot vodka
1 orange wedge

Sandi Howard
Indian Wells Golf Resort
Indian Wells, CA

The Terminator

Southern Comfort
Jagermeister

The Undertaker

1/3 Jagermeister
1/3 orange liqueur
Bacardi 151 rum

Build. Float 151 rum.

Three Leaf Clover

1 oz. Baileys Irish Cream
1/4 oz. Jameson Irish whiskey
1/4 oz. Irish Mist

Shake with ice and strain.

Three Wise Men

1/3 Jagermeister
1/3 Rumple Minze
1/3 Bacardi 151 rum

Build.

Thumper

3/4 oz. Tuaca
3/4 oz. Courvoisier VSOP cognac

Pour over ice and strain.

Thunder and Lightening

1 part Rumple Minze peppermint schnapps
1 part Bacardi 151 rum

Build.

Thunder Cloud

1/2 oz. Bacardi 151 rum
1/2 oz. Disaronno amaretto
1/2 oz. Irish Mist

Build.

Tic Tac Shooter

1 oz. Metaxa ouzo
1 oz. Rumple Minze peppermint schnapps

Build.

Tickle Me Elmo

1 oz. Bacardi Limón
1 oz. peach schnapps
1/2 oz. water
1/2 oz. grenadine

Michael Longo
Lyndhurst, NJ

Tidy Bowl

1 1/2 oz. vodka
1-2 drops blue curacao

Build.

Tidy Bowl #2

3/4 oz. tequila
1/4 oz. triple sec
1/4 oz. blue curacao
1/2 oz. sour mix

Shake with ice and strain.

Tidy Bowl #3

1 1/2 oz. light rum
1/2 oz. blue curacao
1/4 oz. 7-Up

Mix and strain. Top with 7-Up.

To the Moon

1/2 oz. Kahlúa
1/2 oz. Disaronno amaretto
1/2 oz. Baileys Irish Cream
1/2 oz. Bacardi 151 rum

Stir with ice and strain.

Toasted Almond

3/4 oz. Kahlúa
3/4 oz. Hiram Walker amaretto
1/2 oz. cream

Shake with ice and strain.

Toffee Apple

3/4 oz. apple schnapps
1/4 oz. butterscotch schnapps

Wendy Foster
Carney's Point, NJ

Tomakazi

3/4 oz. Beefeater gin
3/4 oz. Fris vodka
1/2 oz. Rose's lime juice
splash sour mix
splash cola

Mix with ice. Top with cola.

Tommy Time

1 part Bacardi Limón
1 part Malibu or Parrot Bay
1 part orange juice
1 part pineapple juice
touch grenadine

Tommy O'Connor
College Park, MD

Tootsie Roll

3/4 oz. Mozart chocolate liqueur
3/4 oz. Stolichnaya vodka
1/2 oz. orange juice

Shake with ice and strain.

Top Banana

1/3 Absolut vodka
1/3 white crème de cacao
1/3 crème de banana

Shake with ice and strain.

Topshelf

1 oz. Tanqueray gin
1/2 oz. Grand Marnier
1/2 oz. sloe gin
1/2 oz. orange juice

Shake with ice and strain.

Rory L. Chatman
Norfolk, VA

Topshelf #2

1 oz. Cognac
1/4 oz. Grand Marnier
splash Johnnie Walker Black Label
splash Bacardi 151 rum
1/2 oz. armagnac
splash orange juice

Rory L. Chatman
Norfolk, VA

Torpedo

Carolans Irish Cream
Drambuie
tequila

Equal parts.

Torque Wrench

1/2 oz. champagne
1/2 oz. Midori melon liqueur
1/2 oz. orange juice

Build.

Traffic Light

1/2 oz. sloe gin
1/2 oz. crème de banana
1/2 oz. green crème de menthe

Build.

Tree Climber

1/2 oz. sloe gin
1/2 oz. Bombay gin
1/2 oz. Stolichnaya vodka
sour mix

Fill with sour mix. Shake with ice and strain.

Tropical Lifesaver

1 oz. Malibu
1/2 oz. crème de banana
1/2 oz. pineapple juice

Shake with ice and strain.

Tropical Tang

1 1/2 oz. Bacardi rum
1/4 oz. orange juice
1/4 oz. pineapple juice

Shake with ice and strain. Top with White Zinfandel.

Tuaca Key Lime Pie

1 1/2 oz. Tuaca liqueur
1/4 oz. lime juice

Shake with ice and strain.

Tuaca Toad Lick

Dip "toad" side of shooter in lime juice and then green sugar. Fill with chilled Tuaca liqueur. Lick sugar strip from side of glass and drink.

Turbo

1 oz. Stolichnaya vodka
1/2 oz. Hiram Walker peach schnapps
1/2 oz. Hiram Walker apple schnapps
cranberry juice

Shake with ice and strain.

Turkey Roaster

Equal parts:
  101 Wild Turkey
  Tia Maria
  Baileys Irish Cream
  half & half

George
Santa Monica, CA

Turkey Shoot

1 1/4 oz. Wild Turkey 101 bourbon
1 1/4 oz. Hiram Walker anisette

Float Anisette on top and serve.

Turtle Drop

1 oz. Southern Comfort
1/2 oz. banana liqueur
splash cream

Angela Eagan
Portland, OR

Tutti Frutti Shot

Fill shot glass with chilled Stroh Obstler.

Twenty-Four (24K) Nightmare

1 oz. Goldschlager cinnamon schnapps
1 oz. Rumple Minze peppermint schnapps

Build.

Twilight Zone

1 oz. Bacardi light rum
1/2 oz. Myers's Original dark rum
1/8 oz. grenadine

Shake with ice and strain.

Twin Sisters
1/2 oz. Bacardi light rum
1/2 oz. Bacardi spiced rum
dash Coke
dash lime juice

John Doyle
Philadelphia, PA

Twisted Red Licorice
1/2 oz. vodka
1/2 oz. sambuca
1/4 oz. grenadine
splash 7-Up

Gina Geremia
New Haven, CT

Twister
1/2 oz. Smirnoff Citrus Twist
Zima malt beverage to taste

Eric Traumuller
Avon, CT

Two Fifty Two (252)

1 part Wild Turkey 101 bourbon
1 part Bacardi 151 rum

Build.

Tyson Bites

1 oz. Absolut vodka
1 oz. Southern Comfort
3/4 oz. Absolut Kurant
1/2 oz. Captain Morgan
1/4 oz. Malibu rum
Equal parts:
 orange juice
 cranberry juice
splash lime juice
splash grenadine

Shake with ice and strain into shot glasses.

Richie Goetz
West Haven, CT

T-Zone

1 oz. Bacardi 151 rum
1 oz. sloe gin

Shake with ice and splash of orange juice or cranberry juice. Serve with lemon wedge and maraschino cherries.

Tracy Harris
Queen Sheba Lounge
Philadelphia, PA

U-2

3/4 oz. Midori melon liqueur
3/4 oz. Rumple Minze peppermint schnapps
1/4 oz. Jagermeister

Shake with ice and strain.

Ultimate 1800 Popper

1 oz. Cuervo 1800 tequila
1/2 oz. Sprite

Build.

Upper Cut

1 oz. amaretto
1 oz. pineapple juice

Upside Down Pineapple

1/2 oz. Malibu
1/2 oz. Southern Comfort
dash pineapple juice
2 oz. orange juice

Shake with ice and strain.

Upstarter

1 oz. Liquore Galliano
1/2 oz. Absolut vodka
dash peach schnapps

Shake with ice and strain.

Urban Cowboy

1/2 oz. Southern Comfort
1/2 oz. Jack Daniel's

Urinalysis

2 parts Southern Comfort
1 part Rumple Minze peppermint schnapps

Serve in a test tube for maximum authenticity.

U-Z

1/2 oz. Irish Mist
1/2 oz. Baileys Irish Cream
1/2 oz. Kahlúa

Shake with ice and strain.

V.O. Breeze Shooter

3/4 oz. Seagram's V.O.
3/4 oz. Rumple Minze peppermint schnapps
splash grenadine

Shake with ice and strain.

Velvet Hammer

3/4 oz. Cointreau
3/4 oz. white crème de cacao
1/2 oz. cream

Shake with ice and strain.

Velvet Hammer #2

1 part Grand Marnier
1 part Hiram Walker white crème de
   cacao
1 dash Asbach Uralt
1 part cream

Shake with ice and strain.

Venetian Blinder

1/2 shot Liquore Galliano
1/2 shot dark crème de cacao
Bacardi 151 rum
1/2 shot half & half

Pour Galliano, crème de cacao, and half & half in shot glass (or layer if you like), and float 151 on top.

Michael Rice, Winner
Galliano Bartender Contest
Minneapolis, MN

Very Berry Kamikaze

1/2 oz. watermelon schnapps
1/2 oz. wild raspberry liqueur
1/2 oz. triple sec
dash lime juice

Joanne Martin
Waterbury, VT

Viking

1 oz. Liquore Galliano
1/4 oz. Akvavit

In a shot glass, float Akvavit on top (use spoon).

Viking Funeral

1 1/3 oz. Rumple Minze
1/3 oz. Jagermeister
1/3 oz. Goldschlager

Vine Climber

3/4 oz. Midori melon liqueur
3/4 oz. Frïs vodka
1/2 oz. sweet & sour mix

Shake with ice and strain.

Volcano

1 1/4 oz. Absolut Peppar vodka
dash Rose's grenadine

Build.

Vulcan Mind Probe

1 oz. Metaxa ouzo
1/2 oz. Bacardi 151 rum

Build.

Waltzing Matilda

1 oz. Bacardi rum
1/2 oz. blue curacao
1/2 oz. pineapple juice

Shake with ice and strain.

Wandering Minstrel Shooter

1/4 oz. brandy
1/4 oz. white crème de cacao
1/2 oz. Absolut vodka
1/2 oz. Kahlúa

Shake with ice and strain.

Warped Willie Shooter

3/4 oz. Absolut vodka
3/4 oz. Disaronno amaretto
splash Rose's lime juice

Shake with ice and strain.

Waterloo

3/4 oz. Mandarin Napoleon liqueur
3/4 oz. Bacardi light rum
1/2 oz. orange juice

Shake with ice and strain.

Watermelon

1 part Southern Comfort
3/4 part Absolut vodka
splash grenadine
2 parts pineapple juice

Shake with ice and strain.

Watermelon #2

1/3 Midori melon liqueur
1/3 Absolut vodka
1/3 cranberry juice

Shake with ice and strain.

Watermelon #3

1 part Southern Comfort
1 part Midori melon liqueur
2 parts pineapple juice
splash grenadine

Shake with ice and strain.

Watermelon Crawl

1/3 oz. Midori melon liqueur
1/3 oz. vodka
2/3 oz. sweet & sour mix

Mix with ice and strain into a shot glass.

Carol Welby & Mike Adkins
Harold Dean's Saddle Saloon
Pueblo, CO

Wave Breaker

3/4 oz. Finlandia vodka
1/2 oz. Cointreau
1/8 oz. Rose's lime juice
3/4 oz. Coco Lopéz cream of coconut

Blend with ice and strain.

Wayne's World or 2000 Flushes

1/2 oz. Smirnoff vodka
1/2 oz. Bacardi light rum
1/2 oz. Midori melon liqueur
1/2 oz. blue curacao
splash peach schnapps
sweet & sour mix

Wane Sparks
Carney's Pt., NJ

Weasel Water

1 oz. Baileys Irish Cream
1/2 oz. crème de banana
1/2 oz. cream

Shake with ice and strain.

Week at the Beach

1 1/2 oz. DeKuyper Peachtree schnapps
1/4 oz. Finlandia vodka
1/4 oz. cranberry juice
1/4 oz. orange juice

Shake with ice and strain.

Wench

3/4 oz. Disaronno amaretto
3/4 oz. Captain Morgan Original spiced
  rum

Build.

Wet Dream

3/4 oz. crème de noyaux
3/4 oz. CocoRhum
3/4 oz. Bacardi light rum
1/2 oz. pineapple juice

Shake with ice and strain.

Wet Dream #2

1/3 Liquore Galliano
1/3 Cointreau
1/3 orange juice

Shake with ice and strain.

Wet Spot

1 part Cuervo tequila
1 part Baileys Irish Cream

Build.

Whatchamacallit

1/4 oz. Godiva liqueur
3/4 oz. Frangelico
3/4 oz. Tuaca liqueur

Claude Levert
Las Vegas, NV

Whiplash

1 part Romana black sambuca
1 black licorice Twizzler

Put the Twizzler in a test tube, then fill the tube with black sambuca. Refrigerate and let the licorice soak up the liqueur. The proper technique is drink the shot and chew on the licorice that has been soaking.

Whirly Bird

Southern Comfort
Chambord
Midori melon liqueur
pineapple juice

Equal parts. Shake with ice and strain.

Alan Smith
Bennigan's
New Brunswick, NJ

Whisker Run

3/4 oz. Jack Daniel's
1/4 oz. Coke
3 drops Tabasco
2 pinches black pepper

Troy Hicks
Brookings, SD

White Cap Shooter

1 oz. Frangelico
top with Baileys Irish Cream

Build.

White Delight

1/2 oz. Dr. McGuillicuddy's Mentholmint
   schnapps
1/2 oz. white crème de cacao

Build.

White Elephant

1 oz. Smirnoff vodka
1/2 oz. white crème de cacao
1/2 oz. cream

Shake with ice and strain.

White Out

3/4 oz. Rumple Minze peppermint schnapps
3/4 oz. Baileys Irish Cream

Build.

White Satin

3/4 oz. Tia Maria
1/2 oz. Frangelico
1/2 oz. cream

Shake with ice and strain.

White Spider

1 oz. Stolichnaya vodka
1 oz. crème de cacao

Shake with ice and strain.

Wicked Stepmother

1 oz. Absolut Peppar vodka
1/2 oz. Disaronno amaretto

Shake with ice and strain.

Wild Hawaiian Turkey Shooter

1/4 oz. Disaronno amaretto
1/4 oz. Southern Comfort
1/4 oz. Wild Turkey 101
1 oz. orange juice
1 oz. pineapple juice

Shake with ice and strain.

Wild Irishman

3/4 oz. Wild Spirit
3/4 oz. Irish Cream liqueur

Shake with ice and strain.

Wild Orgasm

1/2 oz. Wild Spirit
1/2 oz. Devonshire Irish Cream
1/2 oz. amaretto

Wild Peppermint

3/4 oz. Wild Spirit
3/4 oz. peppermint schnapps

Shake with ice and strain.

Wild Sambuca

2/3 oz. Wild Spirit
1/3 oz. white sambuca

Shake with ice and strain.

Wild Thing

1/2 oz. apricot brandy
1 oz. Finlandia vodka
7-Up

Stir. Top with 7-Up.

Windex

4/5 oz. vodka
1/5 oz. Parfait Amour

Windex #2

1/2 blue curacao
1/2 Absolut vodka

Build.

Zimbabwe

1 oz. Absolut Kurant vodka
1/4 oz. orange juice
1/4 oz. pineapple juice
1/4 oz. cranberry juice
1/4 oz. grapefruit juice

Shake with ice and strain.

Zipper

1/3 oz. Grand Marnier
1/3 oz. tequila
1/3 oz. cream

Zipper Dropper

1/3 oz. Kahlúa
1/3 oz. white crème de cacao
1/3 oz. green crème de menthe

Zipperhead

1 part Absolut vodka
1 part Chambord
2 parts soda water

Shake with ice and strain. Top with club soda. Suck up through a straw.

Zombie

1 part Myers's Original dark rum
1 part Appleton Jamaican rum
1 part apricot brandy
3 parts pineapple & orange juices

Shake with ice and strain.

43 Nutty Russians

1/3 Licor 43
1/3 Disaronno amaretto
1/3 Absolut vodka

Layer into your favorite size shot glass.

Frank Lippay
Lehighton, PA

69er

1/3 oz. crème de banana
1/3 oz. white crème de cacao
1/3 oz. Baileys Irish Cream

95 North

1/2 oz. orange curacao
1/2 oz. DeKuyper Peachtree schnapps
1/2 oz. Midori
1/2 oz. amaretto
1/2 oz. Absolut vodka
splash sour mix

Tami Parker
Deland, FL

369

Your Shooter Recipes:

an extra twist. Poppers are similar to tequila slammers in that you slam them down on the bar, but Poppers blow their tops after slamming which really draws attention and the disposable shooter glass makes for quick, easy sales.

Poppers are made to sell on impulse. The Popper starter kit comes with 200 Poppers, lids, pour tops, instructions, posters, and a Popper rack so that a server can walk around your establishment and sell directly to your patrons. For more information on Poppers, or for a free sample kit, call Top-Shelf Marketing at 1-800-766-1695, or visit their website at www.top-shelfmarketing.com.

Test Tube Shooters

Originated many years ago in Canada with glass test tubes, these shooter tubes now come mostly in plastic and in a variety of sizes and colors. Test tube shooters are now a staple for many bars and have gone from a fad to an accepted medium to serve shots and shooters. The most popular way for bars to serve test tube shooters is with a specially designed server or shooter girl (or guy). These shooter girls circulate through the crowd and offer patrons a variety of shooters with many classic and unusual shot recipes found in this book.

One of the main sources for test tube shooters is Top-Shelf Marketing. Their line of shooter products combined with this book is a great formula for success in the shooter business. You can call 1-800-766-1695 or visit www.top-shelfmarketing.com.

The Definitive Guide to Shot Glasses
by Mark Pickvet

Here's the long-awaited sequel to Pickvet's popular book, *Shot Glasses: An American Tradition*. It contains much new historical information and line drawings of shot glasses not shown in the first book. Hundreds of shot glasses are shown, with little duplication of information or drawings. This book is a must for all tumbler collectors. A helpful glossary and value guide are included in the book. *The Definitive Guide to Shot Glasses* is available directly from Antique Publications. Antique Publications, P.O. Box 553, Marietta, OH 45750-0553 or call them at 1-800-533-3433, or fax to 740-373-6917.

Poppers
If you go to a bar and see "exploding" shooters, it's got to be Poppers, one of the many shooter sensations available from Top-Shelf Marketing.

Poppers are specially designed plastic shot glasses with lids. You combine one of the many Poppers recipes like tequila and champagne or schnapps and seltzer and put the lid on the Popper. You then slam the Popper on the bar or shake it and the lid blows off with a loud POP! They're fun, unusual, and inexpensive enough to give away with every sale.

Poppers were developed by George Borrello at Top-Shelf Marketing. In an effort to create something new and unusual, he and his staff came up with the idea of making a tequila slammer with

About the Author

Ray Foley has been a bartender for more than twenty years. He is the publisher of *Bartender* magazine and the author of *Bartending for Dummies* and *The Ultimate Little Martini Book*. He has appeared on *Good Morning America*, *Live with Regis and Kathie Lee*, and countless other shows. Ray resides in New Jersey with his wife and partner, Jaclyn.